WALKING IN THE FOOTSTEPS
OF THE MASTERS

RONIT GABAY

Dear Mike
with Love and Gratitude

Ronit Gabay

Joshua Tree
Publishing

WALKING IN THE FOOTSTEPS OF THE MASTERS

RONIT GABAY

JoshuaTreePublishing.com

• Chicago •

Scripture Quotations (see footnotes in Reference Notes:)

The New English Bible, copyright © Cambridge University Press and Oxford University Press 1961, 1970. All rights reserved.

Holy Bible, New International Version®, NIV® Copyright © 1973, 1978, 1984, 2011 by Biblica, Inc.® Used by permission. All rights reserved worldwide.

ISBN 13-Digit: 978-1-941049-22-8

Book Cover Author Photo: Madeline Vite Madphoto.com

Disclaimer:
This book is designed to provide information about the subject matter covered. The opinions expressed in this book are those of the author, not the publisher. Every effort has been made to make this book as complete and as accurate as possible. However, there may be mistakes both typographical and in content. Therefore, this text should be used only as a general guide and not as the ultimate source of information. The author and publisher of this book shall have neither liability nor responsibility to any person or entity with respect to any loss or damage caused or alleged to be caused directly or indirectly by the information contained in this book.

Printed in the United States of America

DEDICATION

This book is dedicated to the memory of my beloved mother,
Brurya Gabay, who went to Heaven in 2013
during her last visit in the United States.
I am very privileged to have you as a mother.
We didn't share the same values or had the same goals,
and yet you showed me unconditional love,
so I can follow my truth and live my life.
Your legacy can be summarized in one sentence:
"I don't care what puts a smile on your face
as long as you are smiling."

Mom, I am smiling.

TABLE OF CONTENTS

FOREWORD

Rev. Dr. Charles D. Geddes

I have been in ministry for 45 years as a pastor, teacher and spiritual counselor and have led countless workshops devoted to honoring body, mind and Spirit. My association has been with the Centers for Spiritual Living, founded by Dr. Ernest Holmes (Science of Mind®). It is a teaching of building bridges of understanding of all of our great faiths and above all, looking at what we have in common.

The Science of Mind teachings also hold us individually accountable for the life we create and the choices we make. Ultimately it is about the stories we carry forward and coming to a place where our story must be one of inspiration, empowerment, and LOVE; no matter what we may have experienced.

It is about our individual relationship to Spirit, however we may define it, and realizing our great quest in humanity is to finally understand that we all come from the same "soul stuff." It's never about what we **name** it, rather how we **feel** it and conduct our lives with compassion, love, and care for self, one another and our planet.

I currently have a Spiritual Wellness Center in Ft. Lauderdale, Florida, called Bridges of Wellness. We are bridging mind and heart and when I first met Ronit Gabay, it was an immediate heart connection. Hearing her story was a moving testament to her pure intention to follow her "heart song" *no matter what it required*. Her story is one of great courage, perseverance and above all, LOVE. She has what I would call "a passion for the Divine."

"We must be willing to let go of the life we have planned, so as to have the life that is waiting for us." ~ Joseph Campbell

This Joseph Campbell quote appears in her first chapter and it mirrors Ronit Gabay and the fact she consistently chooses to step out of her comfort zones and into the great unknown with faith and trust.

I personally have made choices throughout my life that required letting go of everything as I knew it to begin anew. I believe the spiritual quest requires that and no matter what, the valleys or seeming losses at any time, the true reward is looking back and knowing you made the right choice to grow and evolve as a soul.

Ronit is young in age, but I believe she is an old soul. She was born with an independent spirit and inner guidance to step out beyond the traditional structure of family, tradition and religion.

It was also her quest to see the commonality of the pathway that all the Master Teachers have walked, Moses, Mohammad, Buddha and Jesus and how each of us to grow spiritually, must have the courage to "walk in their own footsteps" and continue to create new horizons of insight and inspiration.

The research required to bring this book into form has taken years and has been immense. Everything that Ronit speaks about in her book, she has sought with all her heart to follow.

She stepped out of her traditional Judaic roots in Israel and moved to America without any pre-conceived plan. With just her innate courage to say "I must do this" gives all the more credibility to her work. Ronit has something compelling to say to everyone who may be at a place of re-examining their life and purpose.

I am privileged to have been asked to do this Foreword. I believe there are 2 great bridges we must cross on this spiritual journey – though there are infinite bridges before us. However, the bridge from mind to heart is the key and from that point the bridge we build from heart-to-heart. Ronit Gabay is a bridge builder and challenges you to go deeper into your core belief. She will open your mind and you will want to share with others the profound insights she brings forth. She enables us to see the sacred path we are all on.

Ronit charges us individually and collectively to be a part of the evolution of earth. Currently we are in an identity crisis on our planet. It demands that we step out of old paradigms and that we are willing to be inquisitive about the values and stories we have inherited.

I believe Ronit poses three great questions throughout her writings:

1. Am I truly living the life that defines my authentic self?
2. Are my beliefs and stories empowering self and others?
3. Am I really willing to be a spiritual explorer and cross new frontiers of knowledge and insight.

Ronit Gabay is a true spiritual explorer. The life that we are all waiting for is in our midst and asks that we have the courage to claim it and live it. Ronit...you have claimed it and you are magnificently living it! Countless lives will be blessed by the stories you carry forward.

Rev. Dr. Charles D. Geddes
Bridges of Wellness
Ft. Lauderdale, FL
www.bridgesofwellness.com

Author's Note to Readers

This book wishes to take the readers through the spiritual and mystical experience of the Masters. Their journey highlights the process of "self" discovery to inspire and facilitate our own spiritual healing. The purpose of this book first and foremost is healing. It wishes to educate people about spiritual healing that begins through the process of seeking inner truth, and it ends with the creation of a new life based on the newfound truth. This process is illustrated through the Masters' lives as it is described in the scriptures and modern sources of information. The ideas presented in this book is to inspire readers to become aware of their own spiritual journey and raise questions that are relevant to their own lives.

The author of this book is not an expert on the subject of religions, and this book is not the kind of book that educates people about world religions. The author is inviting the readers to take this journey along with the Masters.

The author decided to write the Masters' inner thoughts in first person, in italics, throughout the entire manuscript, to emphasize the sense of discovery.

The author wishes to clarify that these inner thoughts are not the original quotes from the scriptures or from any other source of information. The author simply chooses to communicate inner thoughts as she imagined them saying, while experiencing awakening.

With that said, let's begin our journey of self-discovery.

Ronit Gabay

Introduction

A Journey of "Self" Discovery

E arly in my life, I began to question my Jewish faith, realizing that the religious values I was born into didn't align with my inner truth. I tried to fit in and accept my destiny as a Jewish woman, but I gradually broke away, redefining my spiritual identity.

Questioning my faith was a long process, starting back in Israel when my family adopted a religious life, and I didn't follow its logic. In particular, what I found most challenging to accept was the Jewish idea of God, The Supreme Being that sits on His throne making a checklist of all my good and bad choices, and giving scores on the quantity of Mitzvoth I performed, while demanding that I worship Him without question. The lifestyle I had witnessed from my own family made me an odd duck unable to fit in.

One eye-opening moment occurred when I was teaching in a Jewish school in New York, performing the blessing over the bread and thanking God for His creation. In that moment it suddenly struck me that humans were not being credited for their efforts to make bread out of a grain of wheat, and this didn't make sense—because deep down, I believe that people are the vessel through which God is creating the world. And yet, I was still making a living from teaching Jewish culture, conducting prayer and rituals in order to be part of the Jewish community, a path that I was destined to live ever since I was born into a Jewish family.

My resistance to accept the logic of worship and prayer only increased while working in a Jewish school and living in America, but I particularly struggled with my wish to discover the non-Jewish world around me. It took me five years of living in the United Start to cross this forbidden line and go against the Jewish concept of the Chosen People that only leads to intolerance and fears for no good reason.

Everything that I was taught to believe was going against the way I wanted to live my life. I finally announced my liberation from Judaism, wishing to live my truth.

Ironically, my spiritual quest began when my religious experience ended. I was free to be me. And yet, the absence of spiritual content in my life compelled me to ask questions and pursue a deep longing to learn about the essence of spirituality beyond religion and seek a spiritual direction that would make more sense to me.

Surprisingly, I turned to the Scriptures for an answer and conducted elaborate research into the world's religions. For that purpose I researched both the Old and New Testament, using modern text as well as the old King James Version. I also read the Koran and the Hadith, and I used the Dhama-Vinaya to study the life of Buddha. I expanded my research to include newer writers and scholars on the subject to include historical evidence.

As soon as I realized that the Scriptural words of wisdom stemmed from the life experiences of the Masters who spoke them, I committed myself to learn more about each of their lives. This book was born from my desire to understand the journey of "self" discovery that was taken by the great teachers: Muhammad, Jesus, Buddha, and Moses.

The Masters immersed themselves in a journey of looking inward to seek inner truth. The steps that I highlight in this book show that they learned how to identify their inner truth and were transformed through it. Their teachings communicate the message that is found through their inner truth. Their legacy is what we call religions, but the journey itself is a spiritual journey, discovering of the divine quality from within.

I soon realized that the essence of the divine we are seeking isn't an outside source like the God I was taught to believe in, but rather a divine quality, through which we are destined to improve and create the quality of life.

This book is focused on the spiritual experience of seeking inner truth, so we can understand our life mission and the legacy that we will leave behind. When we do so, we will rise to the level of creator whose purpose is to create the world in our own spiritual image.

The journey of "self" discovery starts from seeking inner truth, as we seek the core value that we not only believe in but we must live by. Our inner truth is known in Hindu tradition as *Dharma*. The Sanskrit word, *Dharma,* is explained as the regulator of the Universe, the natural law. It essentially means that all creatures have a natural path that determinates their behavior and choices. It is easy to see it in nature: birds fly, dogs bark, bunnies hop—all of which are natural ways of behaving and natural styles of living. This natural way is exactly how we can explain Moses' acts of interfering to defend the weak, or Jesus' act of love and compassion toward sinners. It's their *Dharma*, their natural state of mind. We can apply the same logic about ourselves: we all have a core value that we strongly believe in, and it dominates the way we behave and influences the choices we make in our lives. It is the driving force behind our actions.

If we only observe our own actions and understand why we tend to react in a certain way or choose a certain experience, we will be able to become aware of our *Dharma*. Therefore, the only way to know the *Dharma* is to seek the evidence of truth, through the process of looking inward.

I was only six years old when I read a short story written by Jonathan Geffen, called "The Green Man." It was about a green man who lives in a green country, and one day he meets a blue man. This story had shattered my life, because I started realizing that I lived in a Jewish country and didn't know any non-Jews. I became obsessed with meeting someone different. "The Green Man" was the catalyst that led me to seek information about the lives of other people in the world, first from geographic magazines, then from my immigrant friends. Eventually, I became aware of my truth, the need to interact with the world beyond my Jewish surroundings. As a result, I chose to live in America, where my inner truth aligned with my life choice. The truth that I discovered was not part of the collective truth that I was brought up with; yet, it is my soul's essence. We are meant to discover the truth throughout our life.

Our inner truth is often contradicting to the external truth that we absorb from our surroundings, mostly because we acknowledge it through a conflict that motivates us to question and seek new direction. In all of the stories about the Masters I have researched, I found that the collective truth they had been introduced to from birth was not the truth that they chose to embrace later on in their lives. Their actions of resistance led them to realize their own inner truth. Muhammad's inner truth is financial justice and balance, driven from his actions to help the poor, and Jesus' tendency for love and compassion stems from his actions to support sinners. Moses' sense of justice was formulated by his actions of defending the weak, and Buddha's essence of liberator was driven from his attention to see suffering. The Masters broke away from the collective truth, and as a result, they created a new life based on their inner truth. But that is not all. Their inner truth formulated their new identity as they paved the way for new direction.

Muhammad became the founder of Islam. Jesus, after his time, was the inspiration for Christianity. Moses, who was brought up Egyptian, became a Hebrew. Buddha, who broke away from Hinduism, became the founder of Buddhism.

The Masters' journey is our journey. We too are seeking to liberate from the collective truth in order to formulate our own identity. Yet, not all spiritual journeys lead to the foundation of a new religion, but it certainly leads to a new definition of self that is created by our own choices.

The Hindu tradition illustrates this with a beautiful metaphor. In every lifetime we wear a different outfit that defines our societal belonging and influences our life choices, but under the outfit is our true self. When we are finally connected with our true selves, we become aware of our unique life's perspective that distinguishes us from the "crowd," and we will take the life path that fits and supports it. The benefit of this journey is that we will take the "right path" that is customized only for us. When we stop continuing to carry on tradition that was established before us, we will be able to create and start something new.

The outcome of the spiritual journey is to enhance our divine quality as human beings, that is changing lives simply by living our truth. Yet, often our daily life struggles, conflicts, and challenges for survival slow down the process and sometimes sabotages it. As we become aware of our inner truth, we are able to make life choices that eliminate those hurdles from our path and become clearer on the direction that our soul desires.

My hope and goal for this book is that it inspires you to liberate yourself from these obstacles and fears, gradually evolving into the higher being as a *creator*.

The seven-step journey, highlighted through the Masters' journeys, is illustrated through the metaphor of a spiral staircase, which I borrowed from author Karen Armstrong. Every time we take another turn, we conclude a spiritual chapter in our lives, learning our life lessons. Every round of the journey completes one aspect of our growth that leads us to the next level, which is more complex and advanced than the previous one. Our spiritual growth is like the growth we gained from schooling. The first phase of the journey is seeking truth equal to the level of "elementary education" where we develop a special sense of self; the second phase of transformation is similar to the level of "high school education" where we achieve awareness about our divine potential, and the third phase of creation is like "academic education" which prepares us to develop the craft and the expertise as a *creator*.

When we acknowledge that we have the higher power of the divine to create the world in our own image, we activate our Godlike potential.

PART I

SEARCHING FOR THE TRUTH

Truth is not something outside to be discovered,
It is something inside to be realized.
~Osho

CHAPTER 1

GOING FORTH:
THE ODYSSEY BEGINS

We must be willing to let go of the life we have planned,
so as to have the life that is waiting for us.
~Joseph Campbell

Home is a place where we feel safe and secure, surrounded and protected by people we love. The home environment introduces us to certain truths and beliefs that we agree to accept. These truths formulate the conditions and values that we agree to live by. As we grow up, we step out from the nest to explore life and start our independent journey. The process is exciting and promising, and it holds the potential for us to learn and evolve.

It is natural to accept the norms of our formative surroundings and embrace the path established for us. We commit to creating a life based on the mindset we inherited, in large part, so that we can be part of the core group we are born into. We follow this route because we want to feel accepted and to belong to our tribes. However, holding on to these "inherited truths" also obligates us to continue the path of tradition that was established before us. If we continue to walk in the established path we become followers, but if we dare to question these truths, we will pave our own path, leading us in a new direction. For example, if we are presented with the custom that everyone must wear black and white clothing, and one day we discover colors, we begin questioning the logic of this truth, which eventually motivates us to accept change, embracing a different truth. At this point, we ask ourselves: which truth makes more sense to us? The truth that is aligned with our hearts is *our* truth. Therefore, the more open we are about new experiences, the more information we will collect about the true nature of our souls.

Leaving home, in a physical sense, is a natural phase of life that happens easily when we are young, but as adults we are hesitant to uproot ourselves and change locations. This is even harder when we have a family and have to consider the implications of this move for them. Yet, the act of going forth can be achieved through the emotional and mental effort to disconnect from the given mindset, cutting the "umbilical cord" that connects us strongly to our family, our tribes, and our cultures' mindset. We are not obligated to accept the "truth" that we are presented with by our tribes.

The act of going forth is usually stimulated by a conflict with our upbringing when we disagree with a truth that was presented to us. It is similar to the normal phase in adolescence when one day the rules in the house are not making any sense. In spite of the chaos, it is a sign of maturity and courage to pave its own path. Therefore, it is natural for us to rebel against the norm, because something does not make sense to us anymore. Our soul refuses to accept the "truth" as it has been handed to us, when deep down we feel otherwise. This sense of "knowing" stimulates our desire to question our lives as is—and own only the truth that makes sense to us. It would be unnatural for us to behave in a way that does not fit our soul.

When we recognize that our birth truths are in conflict with what we feel in our hearts, we know it is the time to "leave" and go forth. Once again, we don't have to leave physically, but mentally, we must separate from the influence of our upbringing so we are able to acknowledge our own truth. By doing so, we don't deliberately hurt the people we love or betray their values, even if it appears this way. We are merely honoring our own truth. The people we love will accept us the way we are, especially when we are at peace with ourselves. We must be free to follow our own path. Going forth is a normal phase of life, which indicates our maturity to evolve. Throughout the maturation process, we naturally begin to question our lives and discover our own essence.

Going forth is precisely the path that marks the life journey of the Masters, as we will learn from this chapter. The Masters didn't find the peace they desired within their birth surroundings, and although they tried, they were unable to fit in. Moses struggled to live in an oppressive regime that didn't honor justice or give respect to people regardless of their background or social stature. Muhammad struggled to accept the social injustice that was created by the wealthy toward the poor; he conducted a kind way of life, reaching out to everyone in need. Jesus didn't accept the measurement of judgment that everyone gets what they deserve by law; instead, he proposed that people should act upon the measurement of compassion and love, first and foremost. And Buddha could not continue to live as a prince once he had witnessed the suffering outside the protection of his palace walls. Each of these teachers had felt that the life they were born into was not the life that was right for them. Something was wrong with the picture they saw, and they felt the urge to go forth and explore a different way of life that would resonate with their inner truth.

The Masters' points of view showed them that they didn't belong in their birth surroundings. They didn't know where or how they would find the place of peace they were searching for; all they knew was that they could not remain where they were.

The first step in this journey of maturing self-realization is to identify what is it that we struggle to accept—what is the point of view that does not make sense to us? And why do we feel unhappy and stuck in the same place? These questions, and more, were carefully considered by the Masters, as they took the first steps to leave their birth community and search for their happiness. Walking in the Masters' footsteps will inspire us to liberate from the values that are no longer making sense to us so we will have an opportunity to learn, evolve, and find happiness.

In this chapter, I describe the unique journey of each of the four Masters as they struggled to accept the truth of their birth surroundings and reached a conclusion that compelled them leave. The act of going forth is, without a doubt, the prerequisite of any spiritual journey.

Step 1: Going Forth

Buddha:
Casting Off from the Warrior Caste, Pabbajja

Siddhartha Gautama was born in 566 BCE to an eminent family in Kapilavastu, to King Suddhodana and Queen Mahamaya. The mother, Maya, had a dream that hinted to her son's future, prior to his birth. As a result, it was said "The world would be flooded with light at his birth,"[1] which prophesied the child's bright future as the new leader. The Queen died giving birth to Gautama.

Gautama's father, Suddhodana, was a distinguished community leader in the Sakya tribe in Kapilavastu. Following Guatama's birth, Suddhodana held a festive banquet in honor of his newborn. He invited a hundred well-known Brahmins to his palace, who were asked to predict the infant's future.

The fortune-tellers differed in their opinions. Some said the boy would grow up to become a universal King, *Cakkavatti*, ruling the entire world, but others said the boy would devote himself to a spiritual life.[2]

The first prophesy was in line with the Gautama's family tradition, which obligated each member to fulfill the natural course of life within the caste into which he was born.

Siddhartha Gautama belonged to the warrior caste, *Ksatriya*, one of a four-level caste system. The levels were: *Brahmin*-priests, *Kshatriya*-rulers and warriors, *vaishya*-farmers or merchants, and *shudras*-laborers or slaves. If one is born to one of these castes, it is expected that they should follow the norm and obligations of said caste. Gautama was destined to be one of the world's greatest rulers, one who would continue to live by the caste obligations, responsible for ruling and protecting.[3] Eventually, Gautama would inherit his father's throne and be a great *Cakravartin* king.

His future seemed crystal clear, yet the path of his life did not go as planned. The second prediction about Gautama's future said that he would follow a simple life, preferring spiritual meaning to a life of wealth. This second view reflected Gautama's potential, which derived from the fulfillment of his true inclination. Fulfilling the path of choice requires paying attention to deciphering clues given by the gods, which would be revealed during his independent life experience. These signs would strengthen his inclination and lead him toward a different destination.

The father hoped to see his son as a leader, a *Cakkavatti*.[4] He feared the prediction in which his son would leave his house in favor of a simple life. Like most fathers, he was concerned about the risks and dangers posed by an unknown journey, and he feared for his son's life. The father listened carefully to the words of Kondanna, one of the *Brahmin*, who warned him against an encounter of four figures who would influence Gautama's world-view.

Suddhodana, the father, then consulted his brother, Dronodana, about the matter, explaining that "The Brahmin and fortune-teller have predicted that my son will become a *Cakravartin* king if he does not leave home to become a wandering ascetic. Therefore, we should watch the Bodhisatta carefully and keep the city well-guarded."[5]

Shortly after this, Gautama's father surrounded the palace with seven walls and iron doors, and he appointed guards to oversee his son's movements. He filled his palace with amusements and luxuries, providing the prince with all his needs so he would have no reason to leave. The palace was packed with fine furniture and splendid plants, which imparted a harmonious appearance. The father hired entertainers to amuse the prince. Beautiful women filled the palace and fulfilled all of Gautama's desires.[6] The father hoped that the luxurious life he provided for his son would assure Gautama's desire to continue the generations-old family tradition.

However, despite the abundance within the palace, Siddhartha Gautama exhibited a natural curiosity about what was happening outside the palace, and as he grew older, he hoped to discover the world outside the palace. His inner wish was heard when the Gods approached Gautama with the great news:

> "Now Indra and the other Gods, knowing the thoughts of the Bodhisttva (one who possesses the ability to become Buddha, the Enlightened One), approached him and said, 'Get-up, get up, well-minded one! Leave this place and set out into the world... you will save all beings.'

> "The Bodhisttva replied, 'Don't you see, Indra, I am trapped in a net like the king of the beasts. The city of Kapila is completely surrounded by a great many troops, with a lot of horses, elephants, chariots and very capable men bearing bows, swords...'

"Indra said: '...You would wander forth from your home. We will arrange it so that you will be able to dwell in the forest, free from all hindrance."[7]

When Gautama was in his mid-twenties, he finally found the courage to ask his father for permission to leave the palace and go into the outside world. The father agreed to send his son to the park and on other occasional outings, accompanied by his charioteer named Chandaka. These outings, however, were well orchestrated by Gautama's service men. They were instructed to remove anything ugly or unpleasant that might disturb the prince's mood. In spite of such efforts, to the father's regret, each time that Gautama became acquainted with unfamiliar scenes of suffering, it further stimulated his curiosity. On his first outing, Gautama asked Chandaka to take him to a particular garden so he could expand his horizon about the real world. On their way they encountered a man bent over with age. "His hair was gray, his face was wizened, his eyes red. His hands shook and his gait was unsteady; he walked feebly, leaning on a stick."[8]

"Who is this man?" Gautama asked his chariot man. "The hairs on his head do not seem to resemble those of other people. His eyes are also strange. And he walks so oddly."

Chandaka replied, "That is an old man. He is that way because of the effect time has on everyone who is born. What that man has is the affliction of old age that awaits all of us. The skin dries and wrinkles, the hair loses its color, and falls out...In fact, as time goes on, our whole body winds up with little strength left, hardly enough to move along."[9]

This explanation frightened and upset the prince. He told the chariot man to go back home in order to escape this reality and return to the pleasant world where everyone looked his best.

On his second outing, Gautama saw a man suffering from disease. "He was emaciated and pale. Part of his body was swollen, and another part was covered with sores. He was leaning on another man for support and occasionally emitting piteous cries of pain."[10] Gautama once again was shocked from the sight, and from the explanation he received.

On the third occasion driving with his chariot man, the prince encountered a funeral procession.

"He saw a corpse being borne on a litter, followed by bereaved relatives wailing, tearing their clothes, and covering themselves with ashes. My prince, do you not know?" asked Chandaka. "The man lying on the litter is dead. His life comes to an end. His senses, feelings and consciousness have departed forever. He has become like a log or a bundle of hay. Those relatives of his who have cared for him and cherished him through his life will never see him again. Without any exception, everything that is born must die!"[11]

It is reasonable to assume that aging, sickness, and death also occurred inside the palace, but the abundance of luxury had diverted Gautama's attention and given him the privilege of enjoying the beauty of life without concern.

The sights of suffering that Gautama had witnessed inspired him to question the life of peace and harmony while the outside world is quite the opposite.

From this point on, Gautama started to pay attention and acknowledge the ugly scenes, even in his own house.

"One night, the prince woke up and saw the beautiful women lying about him, asleep in various positions of abandon. One young woman, who still held her lute, lay drooling from one side of her open mouth and snoring loudly. Other women lay propped against the walls or against pieces of furniture. Some had wine stains on their clothing. Others, with their rich costumes thrown open, lying in ungainly postures with their bodies exposed, looked like corpses. The seductive vision of their beauty, which had so long captivated the prince, was shattered."[12]

That night, the prince had discovered that ugliness and suffering are a normal part of life, one that until now he had been unaware of. In an instant, he became aware that life in the palace was shielding him from the true reality, and he realized that he should learn more about the nature of suffering so he could "fight" it—and find the tools to protect himself, and the people he loved, from such pain. The three people he encountered inspired him to question his own reality, so he could learn and investigate the issue of suffering, which he had become obsessed with.

As soon as Gautama showed an interest in learning about the nature of suffering, the next sign was shown to him. He went out for another trip to a park, where he encountered a mendicant with upright bearing and a serene and radiant countenance. Gautama, who was impressed by this sight, questioned Chandaka about the man.

Chandaka replied, "This is a holy man who has renounced worldly life and entered upon a life of homelessness. Such Homeless devote themselves to the spiritual pursuit of meditation and practice austerities. They have no possessions but wander from place to place, begging for their daily food."[13]

This was the first time Gautama learned about the position of "Homeless," where people from different castes were permitted to leave their caste to seek answers about life's purpose and enlightenment. As far as he knew, he should inherit his father's throne, and he had obligations to his family and his people to continue along this path.

Can I leave everything and go on such a journey? he wondered.

Gautama realized he couldn't learn much about suffering through observation from a distance.

Gautama's new knowledge of a more objective picture of life undermined the world-view he grew up with, and he came to understand the life in which he lived was no more than an illusion protecting him from the truth.

From Gautama's story we learn that once we become aware that the truth presented to us from birth is subjective, and not necessarily the entire truth of how everyone lives in the world, we may feel the urge to venture forth. Gautama understood that he could not live in a place that limited his knowledge and experiences, and that he would rather be free to explore the world outside in order to learn other truths.

Although Gautama wished to leave his palace to learn more about the essence of the simple life, he was still hesitant about such a move. Just as he was ready to consider leaving, Mara, the ruler of the universe, came before him:

> "'Do not go,' cried Mara, 'for, in seven days the golden wheel of universal sovereignty will appear, and you will become ruler over the whole world with its four great continents and myriads of islands.'
>
> "'Mara! I know you,' Gautama replied. 'And, well I know that what you say is true. But rulership over this world is not what I seek, but to become a Buddha in order to heal its suffering.'"[14]

Mara's voice symbolized the inner voice that pleaded with Gautama to follow tradition according to the Hindu caste system. But Gautama expressed his reservation about the destiny that contradicted his will.

Do I really desire a position of leadership which derives from social expectations, or should I develop my own areas of interest? Should I satisfy the social expectations of my caste or should I satisfy my curiosity and my aspirations? he wondered.

Gautama had struggled to accept his responsibility to his family and his caste, so as not to disappoint his family. Yet, he felt strongly that this was not the direction he would have chosen.

Do I have to continue the tradition of my ancestors and make them proud, or shall I strike out on my own and follow my heart's desire? he continued to ask himself.

Gautama wrestled with the social expectations of him but finally decided to respond to the inner voice that urged him to follow his own yearning.

Not long afterward, Gautama made his decision to leave his life in the palace and become a Homeless. In the middle of the night, he woke his chariot man, Chandaka, and asked him to saddle his favorite horse. It was a full-moon night in the summer when the prince left Kapalivastu and went south. After the long distance of riding far away from home, Gautama asked the chariot man who drove him to continue the journey alone.

"Chandaka, I am entering the life of homelessness in order to seek truth for the sake of all. It is time for you to take Kanthaka and go back to Kapilavastu and my father."[15]

He used Chandaka's sword that had been left with him and cut off his hair to give himself an authentic look and erase his previous appearance. Just then, he met a hunter wearing a simple saffron-dyed robe, and they exchanged clothes in order to complete Gautama's appearance as a simple man.[16] Gautama had undertaken an act of *Pabbajja*, cutting the links of kinship and to his native community in order to discover the truth. In an unofficial ceremony, Gautama changed from householder to homeless; he became a caster-off, a *Sannyasin*, which gave him the liberty to wander and do as he wished.

In spite of social expectations that he should follow the traditional path of his caste, Gautama chose to pave his own path. Leaving his palace was a crucial step in following his own bliss. Gautama was not clear about his direction, but he knew he would not find it by staying in the palace.

Step 1: Going Forth

Moses:
Moses' Departure from Egypt

According to the *Book of Legends, Sefer Ha-Aggadah, (in Hebrew): Legends from the Talmud and Midrash,* which provides a commentary to the Bible from the Talmud and Midrash, Moses' sister had a prophecy, probably in a dream, that her mother was destined to give birth to a son who would save Israel from Egypt. When Moses was born, the house was flooded with radiant light. Moses' birth was preceded with predictions about his rule as a future leader, and this was affirmed by a light that radiated far beyond normal.[17] Moses' journey was orchestrated by God from his birth to leadership, so he would fulfill his destiny.

According to the Hebrew Bible, Moses was born in 1525 BCE to a Hebraic family. His birth occurred well after slavery began and during the rule of Pharaoh, possibly from the Eighteenth Dynasty. Pharaoh feared the political strengthening of the minorities in his country and ordered the Egyptians to subdue the Hebraic slaves living among them, saying, "Look, the Israelite people are much too numerous for us. Let us deal shrewdly with them so they may not increase; otherwise, in the event of war they may join our enemies in fighting against us."[18]

Pharaoh engaged the Hebrews in hard labor, and he issued a decree of death against their young in order to reduce the circle of opposition that might rise against him in the future. The Egyptians were ordered to carry out Pharaoh's commands, and they subdued the Hebraic slaves through words and actions. They informed on Hebraic mothers who tried to hide their children and enjoyed a position of power fed by the humiliation of the slaves.

The Pharaoh commanded all his people, saying, "Every boy that is born, you shall throw him into the Nile, but let every girl live."[19]

As a result, Moses' mother placed him in a basket and abandoned him in the Nile River with faith that God would guard her son and would save his life.

The mother's wish was fulfilled when the baby was found by the daughter of Pharaoh, who fell in love with the special baby: "The daughter of Pharaoh came down to bathe in the Nile…she spied the basket among the reeds and sent her slave girl to fetch it. She saw it was a child, a boy, crying."[20] She named him Moses, explaining, 'I drew him out of the water.'"[21]

By all accounts Moses should not have lived, but God intervened. The Bible claims that Moses' destiny was guided by God from his birth because he had been chosen to fulfill God's mission.

The *Book of Legends,*[22] which was written by middle-aged wise teachers, gives us more detail about the story since the Scriptures lack information. One of the difficult questions that the wise teachers were concerned with was why Pharaoh accepted the baby into the household, knowing he was a Hebrew. The legend tells us that Moses was a charming and handsome boy, and whoever saw him could not turn their eyes away from him. Pharaoh, too, used to hug and kiss him. Moses would playfully take Pharaoh's crown and put it on his head.

The magicians were concerned that the boy would one day take the kingdom from the Pharaoh. They suggested a test for Moses to see if he was dangerous to the Egyptian future. They placed before him a vessel with a gold piece and a vessel with a burning coal. If he reached for the gold, he would show that he has the understanding and they must get rid of him, but if he reached for the coal, he was an innocent baby. Moses was about to touch the gold, but the Angel of Gabriel diverted his hand, and instead, Moses touched the hot coal, putting it in his mouth and burning his tongue. As a result, he became slow of speech. From then on, Pharaoh accepted Moses as his foster son, and he never questioned his loyalty. Moses grew up as an Egyptian prince, raised on Egyptian values.

Whether or not we agree with the narrator's explanation regarding Moses' true identity, we know that Moses grew up in the Pharaoh's house, carrying an Egyptian name and identity. Moses never knew about the circumstances of his birth and lived his life as a normal Egyptian, although one who was well connected to the royal family.

As an Egyptian prince, Moses was destined to be a leader. Every day, Moses left his palace to learn about the life of his people. He listened to people's stories and learned about their life challenges. He hoped to use his power to help people and to improve the quality of life in Egypt as a future leader. Moses was well aware of the life of the Egyptian regime, their accepting of slavery, and their policy of discrimination against the slaves. Deep in his heart, this concept didn't make sense to Moses.

Early on Moses had his own mind, unable to accept "the truth" as it was given him. Moses did not follow the example of other Egyptians and did not take advantage of his position and power to humiliate the weak. Instead, he exhibited social sensitivity, which encouraged him to intercede in cases of injustice. Moses gravitated toward people in distress, and his pure emotional reaction motivated him. However, his tendency to help people was not geared solely toward those who were clearly weakened by their place in society, such as the slaves, but for everyone in need, as we can witness from his further actions.

Moses' compassion is illustrated in a well-known incident involving a helpless slave. "He saw an Egyptian beating a Hebrew..."[23] The humiliation of the Hebraic slave invoked the wrath of Moses, who felt compelled to show his resistance to a regime of repression that was perverting humanness. "He turned this way and that and, seeing no one about, he struck down the Egyptian and hid him in the sand."[24]

Defending a slave was considered a violation of the norm. By acting against the norm, Moses expressed his disagreement with the concept of discrimination and humiliation toward any human being. He continued to express his objections through other incidents in his future. Moses eliminated the oppressor; yet, killing the Egyptian did not end the policy of deprivation in Egypt. Moses did not solve the problem of discrimination, but he certainly showed his true nature as someone willing to fight for justice.

In another incident, Moses mediated a quarrel between two slaves.[25] His fervent desire was to solve the problem with negotiation, rather than an act of violence, in order to establish harmony in his surroundings. But everywhere he went, people were fighting, people were disrespecting one another, and the tension was escalating. Pharaoh's policy of deprivation nurtured hostility, and the social situation in Egypt testified to the overall moral deterioration. Moses reached the conclusion that he was incapable of conducting the struggle for justice alone.

To accomplish true and lasting change, a collective effort was needed. The Egyptians, who enjoyed the privileges of Pharaoh's policy, did not constitute a potential coalition for the struggle against deprivation. And the Hebraic community, preoccupied with the struggle for survival, was incapable of defending itself.

Moses was suffocated by the tension he experienced in his birth surroundings. He could not live in a place where people fought to survive. He could not live in a place where people used their power to humiliate others. He could not live in a place where people distrusted one another. He could not live with constant hostility amongst the people.

Moses was isolated in his own surroundings, because he did not accept the traditional values and norms. He didn't belong, since no one shared the same values and no one from his own family or circle of friends would support his view. He had absolutely nothing in common with the people he lived with, not even with the people he loved. He acknowledged that his inner truth was in conflict with the Egyptian reality. He knew he could not ignore the unfairness that was part of daily life. He could not participate in a form of life that contradicted his moral values and inner truth.

Moses lost his own link with the community, and he would never find peace among them.

In his mind, Moses envisioned himself living a life of peace and harmony that could not be found in his birthplace. He longed to live in a place where people respected one another. This wish was probably formulated in his mind long before killing the Egyptian man, but that event was the trigger for him to finally leave Egypt.

Moses' life was also in jeopardy because he had killed an Egyptian to defend a Hebrew slave. During the years I studied and taught the Bible in Israel, I came to believe that Moses left Egypt as a refugee, to save himself from being caught by the Pharaoh's guards for disobeying the king's policy, as is suggested in this quote: "When Pharaoh learned of the matter, he sought to kill Moses; but Moses fled from Pharaoh, he arrived to the land of Midian and sat down beside a well."[26]

In spite of the Biblical evidence, I purport that Moses was a brave man. He did not fear Pharaoh or anyone else. He did the right thing with little concern for his own safety. Moses left Egypt because he disagreed with the norm of behavior, with the policy of discrimination, and with the life of conflict that undermined his peace, not just to save his own life.

In spite of his actions, Moses was unaware of his passion for justice. Moses had no idea where to go or what to do, and yet, he trusted his inner sense of knowing one thing with certainty: he did not belong in Egypt.

Step 1: Going Forth

Jesus:
Walking Through the Narrow Gate

J esus was born in approximately 4 BCE, during the regime of the Roman occupation of Judah. From the writing of the gospels of Luke and Matthew, we learn of a prophecy about his birth. The Angel of God came to Joseph to tell him about Mary's unexpected pregnancy from the Holy Spirit and to prepare him to support her in spite of the fact that they were only engaged and never had an intimate relationship. A similar message was delivered to Mary, according to Luke,[27] telling her about her son's pending birth. The prophecy hints of a unique child who is destined to fulfill an important spiritual role.

According to Matthew, Jesus was born in Bethlehem, during Herod the Great's rule. The fortune-tellers (astrologers) came to Jerusalem to seek the baby destined to become the well-known King.[28] King Herod, who feared the potential of the upcoming king, asked the astrologers to find the location of the baby, Jesus—but they decided to not disclose this information to Herod, concerned for the baby's safety. Later on, an Angel appeared in Joseph's dream, warning him about Herod. Joseph was asked to go to Egypt and wait until Herod's death. When the family came back from Egypt, they went to Galilee and settled in the town of Nazareth.[29]

Jesus, like Moses, was protected by God from the evil king. God continued to orchestrate Jesus' journey and guide him to fulfill his spiritual calling. In spite of the prophecies that hinted to the child's future as the son of God, we can witness how Jesus struggled as a real human being, and how he went through a process of self-discovery similar to what the other Masters experienced.

From the writings of the Roman historian, Josephus Plavius, who lived in 37 CE, we learn that Jewish society was divided into four social sects, each following Judaism in different ways. The Sadducees were the aristocratic, politically-minded people, who controlled the Sanhedrin (the Supreme Court). They believed only in the written law of Moses. The second sect was the Pharisees, who believed in both written and oral law and were the majority of the population. The third sect, the Essenes, maintained a strict ethical and ascetic regimen, which was expressed through their rituals and practice. The fourth sect, the Zealots, hoped for a messiah who would lead them into a political solution against the Romans.[30]

Most theologians agree that Jesus was a Pharisee, a member of the Orthodox Jews, who believed the Torah had been given to Moses on Mount Sinai. The Pharisees also believed in oral laws that added more Mitzvoth in support of the Jewish laws in the Talmud. Jesus sought their spiritual direction and observed their lifestyle, which later on helped him to point out its weaknesses.

Jesus was a passionate student of the Torah and was attracted to the company of the rabbis at the Temple who engaged in the study of the Torah. He demonstrated his knowledge of the Torah during his sermons at the synagogue, and audiences were impressed with his wisdom and astonishing presence.[31]

Despite the congregation being impressed with Jesus' presentation and knowledge, they doubted his authority to be a teacher. "What wisdom is this that has been giving him and how does he work such miracles? Is not this the carpenter, the son of Mary, the brother of James…?"[32] They did not expect him to be the charismatic speaker that he was.

Jesus spoke in public, in spite of his ordinary stature, which naturally showed his courage to be authentic. But Jesus took his actions farther when he expressed his personal opinion about the faults of *Halacha*, the Jewish law, crossing a forbidden line.

Jesus suggested amending the laws of the Torah to address the moral deterioration of his time. He did not denounce the *Halacha* but advocated mending the gap between laws and actions, and the preference for ritual over moral rectification. "Go and learn what the text means, 'I require mercy, not sacrifice'…"[33]

This statement summarized how Jesus objected to the moral deterioration. Until then, Jesus was an average Pharisee who obediently followed Jewish law. But from this point on, he became an outsider who followed his own path rather than that of Jewish law. Jesus' actions took him in a new direction, even though he didn't leave his community.

The Scriptures don't tell us much about the first thirty years of Jesus' life, before he began his mission. The assumption, according to the book, *The Jesus Dynasty*, is that Jesus formulated a strong friendship with his mentor John the Baptizer. The historian of the first century, Josephus, tells us that Jesus joined the Essenes later on, influenced by John the Baptizer.[34]

The Essenes were a small community in a Qumran cave (near the West Bank) who lived in Judah's desert, practiced communal living, and engaged in immersion and fasting rites. The Essenes expressed their yearning for a Messiah, craving change because of the corruption of the moral behavior.[35]

Jesus resonated with this concept since his speeches often pointed out how people preferred to please God with worship while neglecting their moral obligations to help one another. Jesus seized the opportunity to become a messenger and fulfill the biblical prophecy about the coming of the Messiah, so he would have a chance to establish change.[36]

Jesus stayed in Galilee, continuing to preach and heal, and eventually attracted his own community of followers. Jesus' gift of healing made him popular, even among those who resisted him, such as the president of a synagogue, who came to ask Jesus to help save his dying daughter.[37]

The people of the community exhibited mixed feelings toward him. On one hand, they were amazed by his wisdom and charismatic personality, and they turned to him for healing. On the other hand, they flinched at his impudence in breaching the commandments of Judaism and altering the principles of the Torah. Jesus was condemned and shunned by his own people, a community that followed a well-defined way of life, according to traditional principles.

Although Jesus didn't physically leave his birth surroundings, his detachment from the Jewish *Halacha* led to his estrangement from his native community. Jesus did not intend to rebel or change the rules, but he disagreed with the concept of laws that were inflexible. He believed that the fulfillment of the law was not enough in some cases, and that people should behave leniently. His adherence to the principles of love for others and leniency toward their faults provided him with the legitimacy to lead a new way of life, faithful to his own principles.

Disagreement with the norm is the main reason for his breaking away, similar to the other Masters. Jesus, too, took the path of choice. By giving up on his obligations to follow his old tradition, he was able to live by his own truth. He explained his journey with a metaphor, saying, "Enter by the narrow gate. The gate is wide that leads to perdition, there is plenty of room on the road, and many go that way. But the gate that leads to life is small and the road is narrow, and those who find it are few."[38]

The narrow gate is not a bridge to the next world or a reward for good behavior. The concept of reward after this life was developed by Paul the Apostle as a "marketing tool" to attract new believers. However, Jesus didn't talk about a distant future; he preached about the actions needed in the present. It is reasonable to assume that Jesus used the metaphor of the narrow gate to explain the essence of his own journey, choosing his own path, and living according to his own truth.

Taking the path of choice instead of the path of the tradition is a difficult act that invites resistance from the majority, who believe the norm is the only legitimate style of living.

Jesus realized that the traditional lifestyle was less than ideal. He discovered that the *Halacha* was unable to adequately address new problems. He wished to improve Jewish law and bridge the gap between yesterday and tomorrow. But change was a "bad concept" when it came to Jewish law. Even today, Orthodox Jews do not accept any new law, since the Torah is a final product approved by God.

Jesus was one of the few people who chose the narrow gate leading to life, but he wasn't the only one. He paved the way and encouraged people to follow their truth. The wide gate leads all who follow the established path to accept ideas, values, and lifestyle without questioning them. According to Jesus, this path leads to destruction.

Jesus hoped to encourage people to follow their heart's desire and live their truth rather than be followers. Only people who choose the narrow gate will create the change they wish to see in the world. Such people are leaders.

Step 1: Going Forth

Muhammad:
Muhammad's Migration to a New City—Hijira

Muhammad was born in 570 CE in Mecca, a member of the Quraysh
tribe in central Arabia. Muhammad's mother, Amina, heard a voice
during her pregnancy, telling her she carried the lord of the Arabs. She saw
a light glowing from her belly as a visible prophecy that the baby would
have a great future as a *kahin*, a priest.[39]

The motif of Muhammad's birth is similar to Jesus' story, whose birth
was announced to his mother.[40] The same motif, enhanced by a special
light, is similar to Moses' story when his mother recognized that he was
special.[41] In each of these stories, the motif of light highlights the special
child who had been chosen by God to be a leader.

Muhammad's father died during the pregnancy, and then his mother
sent him to live with relatives. His arrival at his Aunt's home caused great
blessings to be bestowed upon the family. His Aunt was able to breastfeed
both he, and his foster brother, and the family was blessed with camel milk
and food, such as they had never seen before.[42]

Muhammad returned to his mother, in Mecca, when he was six years
old, but she died shortly thereafter. After her death, Muhammad lived
with his grandfather, Abd al-Muttalib, and two uncles. The grandfather,
too, acknowledged that Muhammad had a bright future. In a dream, the
grandfather saw a tree growing on Muhammad's back. The top reached
the sky; the branches stretched east and west. The grandfather's vision, and
other stories about Muhammad as a child, predicted the future of a special
man, who was born to serve God.[43]

Two years later, the grandfather died, and Muhammad remained
with his uncle Abu Talib, who raised and loved him as a son.

Muhammad's beloved uncle was Abu Talib, chief of the clan of
Hashim and a respected member of the Quraysh.[44] The two were very
close, and he had earned the people's respect because of his uncle.

The Quraysh tribe settled in Mecca and engaged in trading, which
brought financial prosperity and made them a wealthy tribe. The city
of Mecca attracted many people who migrated for worship purposes, as

they performed the custom of Hujj (the ritual of pilgrimage to pray to the higher God). Many Arab pilgrims came to the Ka'aba (the temple of the Al Llah) every year. Mecca stood at the crossroads of two major routes in Arabia: the Hijaz Road of the eastern coast and the Najd Road. This strategic position gave the Quraysh access to many cities in the region and the power to create alliances with other tribes. By the beginning of the seventh century, they had become very wealthy.[45] Everyone in the tribe held some sort of position in commerce, such as banker or merchant.

Muhammad, too, became a merchant, leading caravans to Syria and Mesopotamia. When he was a child, he accompanied his uncle on business trips, and he learned merchant skills through his traveling. Muhammad also met different people on the road and learned about monotheistic religions from Christian and Jewish tribes. There is no doubt that traveling helped Muhammad to expand his horizons and gather some understanding about the realities of life beyond Mecca. His act of going forth was a gradual process, which allowed him to become familiar with new world-views and to explore other aspects of life.

Nevertheless, Muhammad was a normal human being, and like other members of his tribe, he engaged in commerce and enjoyed economic prosperity, which elevated the tribe's quality of life.[46]

However, the goal of becoming wealthy encouraged members of the tribe to accumulate personal wealth and ignore collective responsibility for their fellow tribe members. Muhammad was disappointed with the social deterioration caused by the greed of such tribe members, who wished to accumulate more money and power. They seemed to care little about their obligation to the weaker members of the tribe, thus dishonoring the spirit of Brotherhood.

The reality of greed and power upset Muhammad, especially since the tribe members could well afford to care for and help one another. He hoped to take advantage of the financial blessings to help minimize the gap and solve social problems within the community. Muhammad disapproved of the native truth that he had been presented, and he kept dwelling on what he could do to change the injustice.

During Muhammad's travels as a merchant, he spent many days alone and frequently spent the night in a cave on Mt. Hira before returning home. Staying alone in the cave gave him an opportunity to channel his thoughts and yearnings for a solution. Muhammad hoped to live in a place where all people cared about one another, helping each other to deal with life challenges, and sharing their material success, so everyone would have an opportunity for success.

Muhammad's journey, and his seclusion in the cave, naturally drew him away from the tribe's daily customs and intensified his longing for a different kind of life. Each time Muhammad returned home, he had fewer common interests with members of his community, and his disappointment compelled him to withdraw.

In contrast to the members of his tribe, Muhammad led a simple life, dressed modestly, and gave gifts to the poor. He became a foster parent of his own slave and took care of his best friend's child to ease the friend's financial burden. He continually helped others in distress.[47]

Muhammad's gracious conduct emphasized his stance as a lover of justice among the lovers of greed in his tribe. He expressed his disagreement with the tribe norms through his actions: He didn't preach to people at this point, but he did the best he could to help people, mostly family and friends; yet, Muhammad knew that the problem was much bigger and couldn't possibility help everyone. He hoped that he would inspire change, leading by example, but people tended to be greedy and egotistic—and consequently, losing their sense of community.

Muhammad continued to ponder how he could establish a sense of responsibility so that people would care for one another. He was obsessed with this question all his life.

At age forty-five, Muhammad began to openly share his vision. In spite of his concern about public opposition,[48] Muhammad was unable to convince many to follow his beliefs. Furthermore, his beloved uncle, who loved and respected Muhammad, remained faithful to the tradition of his ancestors.

Muhammad was forced to leave the city, following the removal of immunity after his uncle's death, which undermined his position and weakened his supporters, who also had to leave the city. Muhammad had no choice but to disengage from his native community in order to survive. He used this opportunity to continue his mission and seek a new audience.[49]

Muhammad's departure from Mecca, known as *Hijira*, was a search for a new path to fulfill his yearning. During his earlier travels, Muhammad had met six pilgrims from the city of Yathrib during the Hajj in 620 CE. They listened to his words, were impressed with his charismatic personality, and believed he was the Prophet. They were not shocked by a monotheistic belief. They had learned of it from Jewish tribes in the city of Yathrib, and they were willing to accept it. They also recognized Muhammad's ability to unite the tribes and establish a new order.[50]

After the death of his uncle in 622 CE, Muhammad accepted their invitation, finding refuge in a neighboring city, Yathrib, which later had its name changed to Medina, the city where the prophet spread his teaching. The people of Yathrib listened to Muhammad and believed in his mission. They also needed an objective leader from outside who could mediate and unite the tribes.

Muhammad realized he could teach the message of God and attract new followers, creating a strong opposition against the Quraysh. In Yathrib, he found a safe haven for himself and his followers who had been forced to leave Mecca as they feared for their lives.

Muhammad did not leave his birth surroundings until his conflict with his tribe became violent and endangered his life, similar to Moses who escaped from Pharaoh's hands. Clearly, Muhammad no longer fit into his community, since he was motivated to live by his own truth.

Muhammad's *Hijira* gave him the inspiration to demand that his followers would perform a similar move. He announced, "...and a man shall have what he intends; so whoever flees from his home for the sake of Allah...his flight shall be accounted for the sake of Allah...and whoever flees from his home for the sake of worldly gain which he aims to attain... his flight shall be accounted for that for which he flees."[51]

The word "flight" hints at the meaning of Muhammad's *Hijira*— *Hijira* means to "cut oneself off from," and parallels the expression go forth. Muhammad called upon his devotees to embark on a flight from Mecca to Medina, to give up their tribal identity, founded on blood kinship, in order to form a new community based on ideology.[52]

In other words, Muhammad demanded that his devotees release themselves from the cultural heritage that shaped their identity in order to assume a new identity.

Breaking away from the old tradition resulted in a new identity molded by a belief system and lifestyle different from the beliefs and customs they left behind. Muhammad set in motion the migration from tradition to a new identity when he called for his followers to disengage from the tribe structure and join a new community founded on beliefs, rather than blood kinship. From this point on, his followers' lifestyles changed. Their tribal beliefs and customs were replaced with new beliefs and customs. His followers would be transformed by their choice to join the new community.

Muhammad proclaimed that whoever fulfills his path of choice, by means of *Hijira*, fulfills the path chosen for him by God. "He who goes forth in search of knowledge is in the way of Allah till he returns."[53]

The chosen path is blessed by God since it leads people to follow their own truth and collaborate with God to improve the process of creation. According to Muhammad's beliefs, God began the process of creation, and human beings have the ability to destroy, or improve, His work.

The Spiritual Lesson of Going Forth

As we can witness, the act of going forth, taken by the Masters, is founded on a resistance to accept the mindset of their birth surroundings. This is precisely what motivates us to take the first step in the journey of "self" discovery, stimulated by a shocking realization that the life we have doesn't make sense to us anymore. Others may honor certain traditions, but we resist them. Others may live according to a certain lifestyle, but we can't accept it.

Until we start questioning our surroundings, our inner truth is just a hidden potential that can only be developed through our future experiences, as we meet new people and discover other perspectives of living that point us in the "right" direction.

I personally experienced this while living in Israel, my homeland, in the reality of conflict between Israelis and Palestinians, which made life there one of terror. People in Israel lived with constant fear for their lives on both sides. I couldn't walk the streets without looking suspiciously at every person who passed me.

I left Israel in 1999, just before the terror increased and, like Moses, I didn't leave my birth land because I feared for my life. I left because I didn't like the deeper truth that wasn't addressed: that conflict only deepened the distance between two nations and ruined any chance for authentic dialogue. I always hoped for a culture of integration, when people from different ethnicities and cultures engage in dialogue on a daily basis. And yet, I didn't know it because I never had an opportunity to experience that way of living. The society in Israel was far from my natural inclination, and my heart was guiding me elsewhere, to seek the place that would fit my essence.

Through my example, I illustrated how my going forth process helped to question the truth as is. This process manifested physically, and I realized my inner truth did not align with my living surroundings. Yet, I didn't leave my country at the beginning of the process, only later on, when I became aware of my resistance. My awareness increased, both by my experiences, which took me away from the truth reflected through my crisis, and the experiences that brought me closer to it.

Seeking the truth is a long journey, starting from the process of questioning and exploring life beyond our own backyard—and accepting changes. When we are finally ready to break free, we are able to question the values that do not make sense, gradually seeking the direction of our soul. As we give ourselves permission to explore the life that is waiting for us, we become open to embracing new opportunities and learning more about different ways of life. The further we go from home, the nearer we get to our true self.

A starter to implement the teachings of going forth:
- Go forth mentally, emotionally, and sometimes, physically.
- Question the mindset—the values and the lifestyle in your birth surroundings—does it make sense?
- Be aware of the "inherited truth" that is still influencing your life.
- Be open to accept changes.
- Be an explorer of life.

CHAPTER 2

LOOKING INWARD: UNDERSTANDING OUR OWN SPIRITUAL TRUTH

Whenever you find yourself on the side of the majority,
it is time to pause and reflect.
~ Mark Twain

Seeking truth is our life mission; yet how can we search for something that we don't know? We have no idea we have a different truth because we tend to accept the truth that had been formulated by our tribe as we learned from the previous chapter. We start noticing the first avoidance on inner truth through a conflict, the same way that adolescent started his journey of adulthood. The questioning process began while we were still at "home" but continues as we experience life beyond the "backyard." Every experience helps us to question our values, comparing the old mindset we raised on with the new that we discover. In fact the situations we experience and the kind of people we meet are influenced by our inner truth on a subconscious level because our soul knows.

How do we know our inner truth?

First, we should identify the core value that influences our choices. We may come up with a list of values that we strongly believe in, which most of those values were taught to us. The one value that we had never learned from others is our core value.

The most efficient way to identify our inner truth is to eliminate the untruth as we ask ourselves what we disagree with. Our core value motivates us to resist and react in a certain way when it is challenged. Therefore, the actions of resistance we are taking against the norm, which can occur in many situations in our lives such as at home, at work, or with friends, communicates back to us the core value we wish to live by. We can't sit still when we witness a situation that contradicts our way of being. It is easier to illustrate it through the actions of the Masters who fought for what they believe in. Jesus, for example, believed in love and compassion, and when he witnessed situations that undermined this concept, he stood up and expressed his objections. Moses was defending the weak and created justice long before we became aware of his role as a leader who established justice. In both cases the actions of resistance indicate the value that had driven them to act according to their true nature.

We all have one core value that we strongly believe in, and when it is absent from our lives, or when it is abused by others, we feel it and take it personally.

The core value is not just a belief, it is our natural state of being. We must live by it, or else our spirit will die. If we resist living by our inner truth, we will experience major crises like depression or a long-term illness, or a chain of crises that compel us to stop living a lie. And yet, living our truth is a hard task to accomplish since often time, our inner truth encourages us to take a position of resistance, rebelling against the norm.

The ancient texts tell us about the process in which the Masters uncovered their inner truth. Each time they witnessed misconduct or sensed a contradiction to their way of being, they expressed their resistance through words and actions. They had to act according to their truth since they couldn't silence it nor live with themselves being in denial.

In many ways, the Masters were rebels, acting against the norm, even though this was never their intention. They only wished to live their truth.

The Scriptures protect the Masters' reputations from being denigrated as "rebels," creating a unique story about the special circumstances of their birth. According to the Scriptures, the Masters were born to fulfill God's special mission, which gave them the right to rebel. They had to rebel and "shake the earth" in order to make an improvement and establish a change. I believe that we all become God's messengers when we stop accepting the truth that we were told and begin seeking our own truth. By walking in the Masters' footsteps, we learn how to pay attention to our own acts of resistance, identifying the opposing view that helps us eliminate the untruth from our lives. This process of elimination helps us find a sense of direction that takes us to our truthful life.

Step 2: Looking Inward

Buddha:
A Free Spirit

Siddhartha Gautama, the prince from the city of Kapilavastu, was born with the potential to become a *Bodhisattva*, an enlightened being.

Gautama rebelled against the caste structure and the social expectations when he decided to leave his family and the life of pleasure he had lived in the palace to discover the essence of the simple life. By doing so, Gautama rejected his status as a householder, one who is responsible for his family. He walked away from his obligations to his community, adopting the lifestyle of a "Homeless," a person who wanders the roads free from affiliation with any caste system, free from obligations and responsibilities, free to do as he wishes.[1]

Gautama wished to investigate the simple life. Even a childhood memory indicated his passion to learn about the essence of suffering, which he revisited later on in his life. Once when he was playing outside as a child, Gautama noticed that a grasshopper had lost its babies, realizing that even bugs experience suffering.[2] This childhood memory stayed with him, offering strong evidence of his inclination to see suffering rather than ignore it. The memorable event from his childhood was a sign from within that showed his natural inclination to pay attention to creatures in distress and identify with their pain, especially notable since his father tried very hard to protect and shield him from any experience of suffering.

It is reasonable to assume that Gautama would have continued to think about the sights of suffering he witnessed from his childhood, but the pleasure and the harmony he was provided at home diverted his attention until the time when he encountered suffering during his visits to the park. These series of events brought back memories and invoked the feeling of compassion that made him question his life, and the understanding that he did not live the life of an average person. When Gautama was twenty-nine years old, after his first son was born, he realized his lifestyle did not suit him.

Seeing suffering while his life was full of pleasure and luxury didn't make sense to Gautama. He refused to accept the norm. He didn't accept the conformist's way of thinking, just because it was the easy or acceptable way to behave. He preferred to take an unknown journey in the forest rather than follow the safe path in the tradition of his caste.

Gautama did not move from one structured reality to another. He continued to live in Vulture Park, where he turned from a prince to a wandering hermit who struggled to survive. He had to look for discarded scraps of food; he had to sleep in the noisy streets; he had to adjust to an independent life without support; he had to get used to a life without servants and learn to accept a harsh life without pleasure. The life challenges he faced as a wanderer invited plenty of opportunities to recognize pain and suffering.[3]

He wandered from one place to another, facing many challenges and experiencing suffering firsthand. He wished to learn the nature of truth about the normal life. I doubt that he had a clear idea of where he was going or what *sangha* community he might join. The signs were revealed to him as he traveled, as Gautama explained:

> "I can recall, Sariputta, how I practiced the four-square practice of the holy life...went without cloth, I licked my food from my hands...I lived on roots and fruits from the forest; on casual fruits that had fallen I existed. I was one who wore coarse clothes; I wore hemp woven in with other things, grave-cloths, dust heap rags. I plucked out hair and beard. I was a thorn-bed man and lay upon a bed of thorn...I lived given to the habit of bathing."[4]

Like anyone would, Gautama missed his family, especially in moments when he yearned to feel loved. He suffered from guilt for abandoning his responsibility to his wife and son. He certainly felt the pain of disappointing his father who had constantly tried to protect him. He also missed the good night's sleep in his comfortable bed and a pampering warm bath.

The memories of the life he left continued to haunt him. He eventually concluded that his suffering was caused by his attachment to the people he loved and his former lifestyle. Yet, he didn't let his memories distract him from his mission. He truly wished to learn about the nature of suffering and wanted more than just a glimpse of it. After all, the only way to find a solution is by knowing the scope of the problem.

Gautama was able to define the cause of suffering (*Dukkha*) throughout his own journey of pain. Suffering is caused by a constant drive for self-satisfaction. We always want more—a better career, more financial success, health, popularity, friendship, love, connection.[5] When we can't get what we want, we suffer. Gautama arrived at this conclusion through his own desire to seek the physical needs that could give him comfort when he was unable to achieve it.

The second, and the main cause of suffering, creates our resistance to accept change, as Gautama had realized: people change, the environment changes, nature changes, living conditions change. Nothing stays the same forever. As long as we are emotionally attached to the past, we will continue to suffer. In order to overcome suffering, we need to release the emotional residue of the past.[6]

Gautama's life experiences gave him the wisdom to identify the problem before focusing on a solution. Gautama realized that suffering is normal and a part of life—yet we don't have to accept it as our "destiny" and can do something about it. Gautama was determined to find an answer to the problem of suffering that seems so real for every human being. Seeking the liberation from suffering was Gautama's inner truth that compelled him to continue his journey.

In the next chapter, we will discuss how Gautama sought even greater knowledge, inspired by teachers. Yet Gautama continued to be an independent thinker; he didn't take things at face value, not even from his wise teachers. He always asked himself the question: does it really make sense?

He tended to doubt any evidence of truth until he could prove it for himself through his own experience. Gautama was seeking the truth within, searching for his own spiritual essence, which we can continue to observe by looking at his later experiences.

Step 2: Looking Inward

Moses:
A Leader of Justice

We don't know much about the childhood of Moses in Egypt as a royal prince because the author of the Torah scriptures gave us minimal information that relates to his rule as a leader. All we know is that Moses was brought up in an aristocratic family, and he was certainly destined for leadership through his connection to the royal family.

Moses could have used his social position for his own benefit. He could have abused his power to satisfy his desires and feed his ego. He could have used his royal connection to influence others for his own benefit. He could have become a spoiled and arrogant man who loved power and popularity. He could have been a cruel leader as he had been taught. But Moses became none of these. Instead, he was a humble human being—quite the opposite of his royal family.

Moses was a "people person." He left his palace every day to interact with people and learn about their lives. He wished to be a different kind of leader. He wished to be one who is sensitive and attentive to his people in spite of the model of leadership he witnessed. From a young age, he paid attention to situations of injustice. He couldn't walk away from people in distress, he couldn't ignore acts of violence, and he couldn't understand discrimination. Moses had high moral standards, which were in conflict with the Egyptian customs, especially toward the slaves who were routinely discriminated against and treated unfairly. Moses did not have a special relationship with the Hebrews; he was not familiar with their culture or their style of living. He simply believed all people, including slaves, should be treated with respect.

Moses expressed opposite points of view from his fellow Egyptians simply because justice was his spiritual truth. This quality was his natural state of being that would be polished through his future experiences, but Moses already possessed this essence.

Moses hoped that in the future he would become a different kind of leader, one who would right the wrongs. But his future leadership was far away, and he couldn't keep his silence until then. Moses had to do something now to change and improve the life in Egypt, saving it from destruction caused by unkindness and humiliation.

However, killing a cruel Egyptian, as he had done, would not stop or resolve the practice of discrimination and deprivation in Egypt.[7] He realized he was unable to make a significant change, but he did not surrender to the Egyptian lifestyle without a fight.

In the incident where Moses mediated the argument between two Hebrews, he asked the offender, "Why do you strike your fellow?"[8] Moses was trying to initiate communication between the two instead of the violent argument. He tried to show a different way to resolve an issue and establish harmony, but the offender rejected his assistance. He saw Moses as an Egyptian and a hostile enemy. He didn't believe in his sincerity to offer help. "Who made you chief and ruler over us? Do you mean to kill me as you killed the Egyptian?" the offender snarled.[9]

The fight between themselves helped Moses realized that the life in Egypt caused tension, suspicion, and mistrust even among the Hebrews. The situations Moses witnessed troubled him. He lost hope for a better future since both the Egyptians and the Hebrews seemed to be involved in hostility, and haters are unable to attend to the kind of changes that lead to harmony. The Egyptians who enjoyed power over others would not surrender their power, and the Hebrew slaves were too busy struggling to survive to consider other ways to live their lives.

The effort by Moses to improve the quality of life in Egypt came to a dead end. He didn't have the power to make significant change, not even as a royal family member. He concluded that he could not live in a society that violated his own moral values. He did not reject slavery since it was a fact of life; nevertheless, he believed all people, including slaves, should be treated with respect—and he certainly did not agree with humiliation and violence.

Disappointed with his life in Egypt, Moses desired to find a new home, one free from discrimination, free from violence, free from humiliation. Moses escaped to the desert of Midian, where he sat down by a well to quiet his mind and consider the future. He noticed seven girls who came to draw water from the well to water their flock. The girls were interrupted by a group of shepherds who took their water and drove them away. Moses could not ignore the act of violence and rushed to help the girls. "Moses rose to their defense, and he watered their flock."[10]

Once again, Moses could not resist defending the weak and resolving their problem. He even watered their flock as an extra act of generosity.

His actions always showed his true nature as a leader of justice. He had this natural ability to see things that other people didn't—and took action to resolve a problem. This quality was part of his essence, and his experiences helped him to develop this quality and acknowledge his gift. Moses was unaware of it, but his actions demonstrated that justice was his inner truth.

Future experiences would help him become more in touch with his inner truth, and the incident near the well had brought him into the right place where he would develop his gift and acknowledge his passion.

The event near the well brought Moses to Midian, where he was invited as a guest of honor by the father of the girls, who happened to be the leader of the tribe. Moses soon was married to one of the seven daughters, and he settled in Midian where he found a peaceful life suitable for raising a family.

The end of his first chapter in Egypt led Moses to start a new life in Midian, where he witnessed the leadership of his father-in-law: leadership founded on justice and respect. In Midian, Moses observed and learned how to keep harmony between people with different interests and how to resolve arguments through negotiation. Moses was able to develop his natural ability as a leader simply by observing a good role model of leadership, which we will discuss in the next chapter.

Step 2: Looking Inward

Jesus:
The First Reformist Jew

The Scriptures tell us that from an early age, Jesus showed an unusual interest in and knowledge of the Torah. During one of his family's visits to Jerusalem at the end of the Passover pilgrimage, the twelve-year-old Jesus remained in the temple while his parents looked for him everywhere. They found him in the company of teachers who were amazed by his questions and passion for knowledge. When his parents confronted him about where he was, he responded, "Did you not know that am I bound to be in my Father's house?"[11]

The temple was a natural place for Jesus to be as he developed a natural inclination to study the moral behavior as it was addressed through the Torah, the Book of Laws. His tendency to learn about morals and to apply them in practice was his inner truth as Jesus sought the company of the wise teachers and hid in the Holy Temple, unwilling to go home to his normal life. This was a normal place for Jesus to be ever since he was a child. Jesus continued to behave outside the norm on many other occasions, following his heart rather than following tradition.

Jesus was aware of his heart's inclination as a youth, which we also found in the story about Muhammad and the story of Buddha. They all found significant evidences from their childhood that exposed their heart's inclination early on. Jesus continued to seek the company of teachers and study the Torah as an adult. He was naturally drawn to learn about morals and self-improvement through spiritual work.

Jesus began speaking in his local synagogue, impressing the congregation with his knowledge and confidence. Yet, Jesus didn't find the Jewish law to be impactful enough to create significant improvement. Soon he expressed his objection to the principles of Jewish law that dictated strictness, especially toward sinners. According to Jewish law, every sinner deserves punishment, which must be measured against the sin. Jesus disagreed with this concept. He pointed out that Jewish law lacked the concept of forgiveness, a concept that could lead to redemption and a positive outcome. Jesus claimed that the Torah was not enough to create an ideal society—and he intended to change the mindset that would lead to a better future.

In the Sermon on the Mount, Jesus communicated clearly his intention to change the old mindset. He did not deny the accomplishments that had been achieved before him, but he wished to add more improvement to the Jewish law, to include a compassionate approach toward sinners and the poor.

"Do not suppose that I have come to abolish the Law and the prophets; I did not come to abolish, but to complete," he said.[12]

Jesus objected to the idea of measure for measure, which he saw as leading to vengeful actions that destroy life instead of repairing it. Jesus claimed that a real change of life should be founded on the true essence of love, which serves as the internal motive for good behavior; it does not depend on law requirements. The outcome of law is obligation, whereas the outcome of compassion is giving.

We don't need a list of laws telling us what not to do. We need an approach that teaches us kindness to one another, he thought.

Jesus suggested loving the enemy instead of resisting him; walking one more mile toward a person in need; giving more, not less, to develop the habit of kindness and awareness of love and compassion. Jesus practiced what he preached as he set out to eat in the company of sinners and gave special attention to the poor.

His intention to change Jewish law sparked a storm of resistance among the Jewish public, especially from the rabbis and teachers who were close to him. They all agreed, as the Pharisee, that the Torah was a final product given to Moses on Mount Sinai and that it did not require human suggestions to complete God's words.

The leaders of the congregation were shocked by the resistance of Jesus to the strict letter of the law. They didn't expect that anyone would undermine the perfection of the sacred book. They were even more shocked when Jesus took the action against the written law, such as breaking the Shabbat rest to heal the sick.

"The Sabbath was made for the sake of man, not man for the Sabbath…" Jesus responded.[13]

In one incident, people complained that the disciples of Jesus picked corn on Shabbat, breaking the law of "do not do any work…"[14]

Jesus defended them, saying: "If you had known the meaning of the text, 'I require mercy, not sacrifice,' you would not condemn the innocent," he told them.[15]

What is the point of satisfying God with gifts and rituals if people disappoint Him with misconduct against another human being? Jesus suggested that people must think with their hearts before judging misconduct. One must put the person in need before himself. Jesus claimed that every person could do this by following a simple lifestyle and avoiding greed and selfish desire.

Jesus encouraged the public to work on the virtues of love and compassion toward their fellow man. He himself insisted on living up to his truth when he healed the sick on Shabbat, which is the day of sacred rest.

"Is it permitted to heal on Shabbat?" Jesus was asked.

Jesus justified his actions in a parable:

"Suppose you had one sheep, which fell into a ditch on the Sabbath. Is there one of you who would not catch hold of it and lift it out? And, surely a man is worth far more than a sheep! It is therefore, permitted to do good on the Sabbath."[16]

Taking the risks and enduring insults from the community were the prices that Jesus had to pay for the sake of love. Jesus rebelled against the Jewish society that refused to accept changes. He didn't wish to break away from Judaism, but he did since he didn't share the same lifestyle or live by the same values anymore. His true essence was giving him the divine quality to make a difference in the world.

Step 2: Looking Inward

Muhammad:
A True Monotheist

Muhammad was raised and protected by his beloved uncle, Abu Talib, who also was chief of the clan of Hashim and a respected member of the Quraysh.[17]

Muhammad used to accompany his uncle on business trips to Syria. On one occasion, the monk, Bahira, welcomed the merchants who passed him and invited them to a feast. Muhammad, who was the youngest, stayed outside to guard the merchandise while the other, Qureshi, accepted the invitation. Bahira studied his guests, expecting to meet the prophet of God among them, but none of them fit the description of the prophet he had read about in his book. Eventually, he asked his guests if anyone else was with them. The Qureshi called Muhammad to join them, and the monk found who he was looking for.

After the meal, Bahira took Muhammad aside and asked him to swear by the goddesses of the Qutaysh, al-Lat and al-Uzza, that he would speak the truth. But Muhammad resented the monk's request and responded:

"Do not ask me by al-Lat and al-Uzza…for by al-Llah nothing is more hateful to me than those two."[18]

Muhammad spoke his mind openly for the first time, expressing his resistance to the tribe's faith. He refused to believe in the goddess of his own tradition. He only acknowledged his faith in Al Llah, the higher God, which was unusual for a Quraysh member. Muhammad was only a child when he openly admitted his faith in Al Llah.

Muhammad, just like Jesus, had discovered the true nature of his soul in his childhood, which reinforces the notion that our soul knows its true nature. No one forced him to speak about his true faith, and no one taught him to claim it. It was Muhammad's strong sense of self that led him to speak his inner truth.

The monk, Bahira, studied Muhammad's behavior and examined his body for a special mark of a prophet. Then he told the uncle, Abu-Talib, to take his nephew and guard him carefully from those who would resist him in the future.

Muhammad grew up to be a kind young man, known as al-Amin, the Trustworthy. He gave people his full attention while talking to them. He surprised others with the warmth of his handshake, and he was never the first to withdraw his hand. Muhammad was a "people person," which helped him in business as he traveled the roads to trade.

In 595 CE, he was offered marriage to an older widow with whom he did business. Muhammad accepted her offer and was happily married. Muhammad had followed the social expectations of his tribe, attaining a financially-sound position, which empowered the tribe's political influence. Continuing in the tradition of his tribe, he married a tribe member. Muhammad started a family. He was a great father and loving husband. Nothing about his life was unusual or different from the tribe's traditional lifestyle.[19]

But Muhammad was indeed different from many tribe members who used their positions to make more money and gain more power. They refused to care for weaker families who could barely feed their children. Muhammad was disappointed to witness the gap between families who lived luxurious lifestyles and those who had no food to eat. He disliked the disparity between rich and poor created by greed and selfishness.

Muhammad was a man of means, and he did his best to help people in need among his closest friends and family. He gave his foster mother, Halimah, a generous gift of forty sheep and camels to assist her in providing food for her family during the famine in the Hijaz. On another occasion, Muhammad noticed how his uncle, Abu Talib, struggled to provide for his large family, and he suggested that he find foster families for Abu-Talib's oldest children, Ali and Jafar, to minimize his burden until his circumstances improved. Muhammad asked his cousin, Abbas, and his uncle, Abu-Lahab, who were successful businessmen, to foster one of Abu Talib's sons. Muhammad had six children of his own, and he fostered his slave, Zayad ibn Harith, and treated him as his beloved son. Yet, he didn't refuse to take Ali under his wings to help out.[20]

Muhammad was well known for his kindness toward the poor and slaves at time when people were selfish and greedy. Helping people in need was, and is, not outrageous behavior, so Muhammad's compassion and kindness did not upset anyone. But he was frustrated by the unjust reality that created tension among the tribe's families who were supposed to help one another as agreed upon in the Muruwah. The custom of Muruwah is a bond of brotherhood founded on the responsibility of each member of the tribe to help one another and maintain a strong unit.[21]

It is true that the Muruwah was designed to offer life protection in a war against other tribes; however, Muhammad had hoped it could be extended to offer financial and social support as well. Muhammad suggested applying the same logic of protection in war to protect people in distress.

If only people could extend their brotherly commitment to offer financial support, there would not be any distress and poverty in the tribe, he thought.

He alone could not help everyone; but together they could establish a new system that would ensure everyone was cared for.

Yet later on, Muhammad expressed actions of resistance openly, realizing he must rebel against the religious beliefs of his tribe that were part of the problem. In 612 BCE, Muhammad took the first tentative steps to make his mission public. Mostly he confided in his close relatives, such as his wife and children, his foster son, his brother, his cousins and others. However, his beloved uncles Abu Talib, Abbas, and Hamazah were not interested.[22]

Muhammad shared his mission with his best friend, Abu Bakr, who immediately accepted Islam. Muhammad said, "I never invited anyone to accept Islam, but all have shown signs of reluctance, suspicion, and hesitation, except Abu Bakr. When I told him of it, he did not hold back or hesitate."[23]

Abu Bakr was Muhammad's best friend and a dream solver, helping Muhammad recruit younger men in Mecca to the Islam faith. Muhammad's teaching appealed mostly to those young men and poor who had nothing to lose. They embraced the idea of social justice because they were the ones who needed it most.

After gaining the confidence of his first followers, Muhammad began pursuing his mission openly in 615 CE with the help of Abu Bakr. He invited forty members of the Hashim clan to a modest meal. At the end of the meal, Muhammad expounded on the principle of his teaching. The meeting was interrupted by a few people who disagreed with Muhammad's ideas. Muhammad hosted another meal the next day, and he again explained the concept of Islam.

Muhammad encountered a storm of opposition against his concept, not because of his teachings against greed and selfishness, but because he introduced a new concept, Judgment Day, influenced by a similar belief in Judaism and Christianity. He claimed that everyone would face Al Llah on the Judgment Day and would have to explain why he or she didn't fulfill God's wish. The concept of an afterlife was a speculation he could not prove.[24]

Soon the Quraysh was divided between the Muslim minority and those who opposed Muhammad's teachings. But in 616 CE, Muhammad almost lost his supporters when he forbade the worship of the daughters of God (in Arabic called Banat of Al Llah). Instead, he insisted, his followers could worship only Al Llah, the one and only God.

Muhammad wanted more than social reform. He wished for a radical change of consciousness that would replace the old faith. This was the straw that broke the camel's back. Not only did Muhammad lose many of his followers, but he also sparked the first blood fight between the Quraysh traditionalists and the Muslim community which, up until then, had been one unit.

As we witness from Muhammad's actions, conflicting points of view highlighted his stand against the norm, which led Muhammad to think about the concept of one God as a revolutionary way to instill change. The actions of resistance stemming from this concept were manifestations of his intention. Muhammad could not let go in spite of the fact that he didn't have a large following or even when his beloved uncle, Abu-Talib, chief of the Hashim clan, did not support his teachings.

The uncle received complaints about Muhammad from tribe members who asked him to withdraw his protection (*awliya*) of Muhammad. Without the protection of the tribe, Muhammad could not survive in Arabia.

"O, Abu Talib, your nephew has cursed our gods, insulted our religion, mocked our way of life, and accused our forefathers of terror; either you must stop him or you must let us get at him…and we will rid you of him."[25]

Abu Talib loved his nephew, whom he had raised as a son, and he wished to protect him. But as chief of the clan, he had responsibilities to his clan, and the clan would be in conflict with other clans if he continued to protect Muhammad. Abu Talib was approached again.

"By God, we cannot endure that our father should be reviled, our customs mocked, and our gods insulted," his clansmen said. This time they threatened to fight them both, even though Abu Talib was not a Muslim.[26]

Abu Talib finally confronted Muhammad.

"'Spare me and yourself. Do not put on me a burden greater than I can bear,' his uncle said. Muhammad replied with tears in his eyes, 'O, my uncle, by God if they put the sun in my right hand, the moon in my left on condition that I abandon this course, until God has made it victorious, or I perish therein, I would not abandon it!' Abu Talib then told him, 'Go and say what you please, for by God I will never give you up on any account.'"[27]

Muhammad did not give up on his mission even though he saw how his own family was divided. He was aware of his uncle's pain when their sons chose to follow Muhammad's path. He knew his life was in danger, but he had no doubts about his passion. He never compromised his truth. He insisted on remaining in Mecca until his beloved uncle Abu Talib died. With his uncle's death, Muhammad lost his protection, and he was forced to look for a new place to live where he could continue to spread the message of Islam.

Muhammad had a different mindset that indicated his spiritual inclination towards balance and fairness, and although Muhammad was not completely clear about it, he knew all along that he could not give up on his truth to please anyone, even his own uncle.

Muhammad was a rebel who demanded that his followers rebel against their own families and the tribe's norm to prove their loyalty to Al Llah and his messenger, Muhammad.

"Whoever sees me, has seen God"[28] Muhammad claimed, carrying God's will.

As we learn from his actions and words, Muhammad became aware of his inner truth through his future experiences.

The Spiritual Lesson of Looking Inward

Searching for our inner truth is an ongoing process that starts at home and continues throughout the majority of our lives. Everyone has a different truth, which is formulated through the core value that we strongly believe in, and we can't possibly live a life that contradicts it. If we witness reoccurring misconduct and feel a strong urge to do something to stop it, it is a great indication that we resist the untruth. As we become aware of our inner truth, we pay closer attention to the missing value that cause detrition, which motivate us to find a solution. Therefore, when we become aware of our inner truth, we also become aware of the purpose and mission we choose to take on in this lifetime.

Our life experiences lead us on a slow and steady path of discovering our inner truth. There are a few measures that help us discover it, which are exemplified by the Masters' journeys. First, there is a childhood memory, since children are naturally authentic and express their spiritual truth through their activities and choices of interest.

As I mentioned before, I, too, was inspired by a children's story to reveal my heart's inclination toward Oneness. This piece of evidence from my childhood was very significant to my choice as an adult to leave Israel and live an integral life in a multi-cultural life I found in the United States. It is part of my *Dharma*.

We are all capable of looking back and identifying the clues from the past that indicate our hearts' inclinations. These memories are evident of knowledge that we possess all our lives. Yet, childhood memory is not the only sign of insight; the second indication is an act of resistance against the norm, which often shows up as a conflict. In spite of the fact that conflict undermines our peace, we have to recognize its potential to help us to communicate our unique points of view, different from those of others around us.

Most times, we focus on the feeling of getting hurt, ignoring the content of the conflict and its meaning. But if we pay closer attention to the essence of the dialogue, we will be able to identify the value that we strongly disagree with, which highlights the core value that we can't live without.

Let me illustrate it with another example about an ongoing conflict with my co-worker while working as a Hebrew teacher in a Jewish Orthodox school. I was an unconventional teacher who encouraged self-expression and creative thinking through modern literature, while my co-worker was a traditional teacher using sacred text only and dictating notes. Although my approach was very successful, the Orthodox way of schooling does not encourage individual expression. My co-worker's style of teaching aligned with the school's concept, whereas mine was revolutionary and daring. This difference between us gave me a deep understanding about my nature as a creative thinker and a free spirit, which I will continue to develop through my future experiences. But, above all this conflict highlights my persistence to break free from tradition, which only made me realize that I didn't belong in a traditional framework like the one I left behind. As long as I keep making choices to link myself with traditional surroundings, I will be going against my truth.

Once we understand our core value, it will be easier to eliminate the choices that are not supporting it and seek the opportunities that will. From this point, we start making conscious choices to align our life choices with our inner truth to improve our lives.

Seeking inner truth is the first part of our journey. Later on we are transformed by it, changing ourselves, our surroundings, and lifestyle to support the person we have become. But the journey does not end there. As we change as individuals, we pave the way for a much bigger change, simply by living the truth and modeling a new way of life.

As we have learned from this chapter, the "rebel" who fights against the norm is the person who brings the message of change into our collective consciousness. He is the person who helps improve life and helps move civilization forward, just as the Masters did. Therefore, "rebellion" is not a curse, but a blessed quality that empowers one to become Godlike and make the world a better place.

A starter to implement the teaching of looking inward:
- Remember a significant childhood memory about your heart's inclination.
- Take a closer look into your conflict to identify your unique point of view.
- Evaluate your action of resistance in order to clarify what you are truly objecting to.
- Knowing what you don't want brings you closer to your desire.
- Identify your spiritual truth.

CHAPTER 3

SOURCES OF INSPIRATION: DIRECTION AND SIGNS

Do not go where the path may lead,
go instead where there is no path and leave a trail.
~ Ralph Waldo Emerson

For the most part home is a safe place to live, which gives us a sense of peace. But when our birth surrounding only gives us stability and no longer provides happiness, or stimulation to grow, it is time to leave and seek it elsewhere. Yet, most people have the misconception that holding on to a familiar situation helps to feel secure and peaceful. Why? Because the other option of going forward to explore the unknown opportunities seems very frightening.

Entering the territory of the unknown is illustrated through a metaphor of entering a wild forest. In the forest the trees' roots are blocking the path and the branches hide the horizon with shade. Without a path on the ground and a clear vision of direction, we can't see where to go. In addition, the forest is a territory where strange creatures and wild animals live. The possibility that we could face unknown and frightening challenges, and meet different creatures, is very real. No one wants to leave home to face the dangers of the forest.

The image of the forest is taken from the historical quest of the knights in the Middle Ages entering the forest to search for the Holy Grail. Back then one could choose if he wished to submit himself to work for the knights in exchange for protection, or he could prefer to be his own master but live a risky life in the forest. One had to choose between freedom and safety. The same question is relevant to us today, even though we don't have to be in an actual forest.

The knights entered the forest to search for the Holy Grail, which is a symbol of inner truth. Once again, the purpose of this journey is seeking truth. The forest has no path because we are supposed to pave our own path. It lacks destination because we create our own destination through our unfolding experiences.

Life is just like the forest, and we are just like the knights who walk with courage, paving the path for our future. We are not alone. The Universe is watching us and guiding our way. The Universe is my choice of calling the higher power, since I believe that the Universe is a calibration of forces such as Angel, spiritual guides, God, and it even includes humans. We are not separated from the source, or the Universe, and therefore I prefer using the term to express this union.

Some of the experiences in the "forest" are challenging and painful, which is part of getting adjusted to unfamiliar places or strange forms of life. This learning process is designed to teach us an important lesson and gain life skills that we lacked before. As long as we are open to learn and accept changes, we will be able to advance. If we are brave enough to take a chance and seek a new direction, the Universe will help us to find our way. Therefore, courage and trust are certainly qualities we need most in our lives.

Every experience we have while walking in the "forest" is like a sign that points us in the direction that is right for us. If we trust it, our inner voice will guide us to find the path. We should learn to recognize the signs and "read" them, just like we read a road map as we travel to a new place.

This chapter demonstrates how the Masters developed a sense of direction, accepting the help that the Universe had sent their way, listening to the directions and noticing the signs. In this chapter, I will describe the unique journey of the Masters as they were guided to meet new people who inspired them to think about new directions.

As we can learn from the Masters' journeys in the forest, the sources of inspiration will appear in a form of experiences and encounters with unfamiliar people guiding us in the direction of our truth. We need only pay attention to the signs and trust they lead us in the direction of our hearts.

Step 3: Sources of Inspiration

Buddha:
Buddha Inspired to Seek Liberation

S iddhartha Gautama now lived in the forest like a wandering hermit, breaking away from the norm and from social expectations.

The forest is a territory of freedom where people do not live by the rules of the nearest kingdom, as it was in the Middle Ages. By leaving his own caste, Gautama broke the rules of his structure by entering the forest with courage. He would learn about the experience of suffering, and about taking responsibility for our destiny so we do not have to suffer. Gautama had no idea where to go nor what to do, but he understood that the first step in finding a solution to a painful problem depends on knowing the symptoms of the problem. Gautama got used to sleeping in the streets, he begged for food from passersby, and he searched for shelter and safety. Suffering these and other experiences of survival, as well as the pain of attachment toward his family and even for objects that brought him pleasure and comfort, taught him about the real causes of suffering.[1]

When Gautama became aware of the pain of suffering, he was ready to consider the option of spiritual practice that was often available to wondering hermits. Gautama spent many days and nights in the streets inquiring about the Sangha, a community of seekers who come together to experience spiritual practice and learn about enlightenment. Gautama wished to join the Sangha communities, where he could study with a Yogi, a teacher, and learn new techniques and gain knowledge about the process of liberation. Gautama arrived at Vaishali to study the *Darmah* teaching of Alara Kalama, who became his first mentor: "Sir, I wish to lead a holy life under your guidance. Please allow me to remain here and teach me your doctrine and practice."[2]

It was Kalama who introduced Gautama to the Samkyha method, which is a spiritual philosophy that incorporates internal and external knowledge for everlasting peace. The foundation of Samkyha is based on the belief that ignorance blocks the way to our true self. The Samkyha technique strives to discriminate between the absolute spirit of one's being, his *Puresa*, and his material self, *Prakrti*, in order to prevent the emotional distraction that blocks intellectual ability. The technique focuses on intellectual effort, leading the student to direct knowledge free from illusions and liberates them from the ego.[3]

Gautama joined the Sangha to answer the question: How can a man avoid emotional distraction and material temptations through intellectual effort?[4]

Gautama was a very enthusiastic student, and he progressed constantly, yet he insisted that the spiritual self is a knowledge that comes from within and not from outside sources, which opposed his teacher's point of view. He believed that a person knows when he is going in the right direction and when he is not, and that one should always listen to his inner voice that shows him the way.[5]

Although he was open to learning new information, he immediately disagreed with his teacher about the nature of the direct knowledge. His teacher claimed that direct knowledge connects a person to his spiritual essence, but Gautama argued that the spiritual essence of oneself exists within. He didn't base this belief on knowledge but on a strong intuition supported by his own experience.

"Why did I leave my old life behind and go on such a journey unless I felt that it was the right thing to do?" he asked himself.

When Gautama established his own Sangha, he told his students that knowledge is not found in the teacher's sleeves, but is the result of the student's free thinking and recognition of his true self.

"O, Kalamas [one of his students], when you know for yourselves that certain things are unwholesome [akusala] and wrong and bad, then give them up…And when you know for yourselves that certain things are wholesome [kusala] and good, then accept them and follow them."[6]

In simple words he said, "I know when it is right, and I know when it is not; just listen!"

This powerful statement is valuable to all of us. We must listen to our inner voice and do what feels right from within.

Gautama became aware of the connection between the *Dharma* teachings and his life experiences. If he couldn't experience the impact of knowledge he was being taught for himself, he could not be sure of its truth.

Gautama argued with his teacher, Alara, that he should add a different kind of practice to connect the mind with the self and develop control on a conscious level.[7]

Gautama was aware of the different techniques of yoga from other spiritual seekers, and he wished to combine its practice in the hopes that it would increase a person's awareness of the present moment. This would free him from distractions such as the ego, desire, and fear, which all block the progress to reach enlightenment. Yoga practice could assist with shifting the focus from the ego to the spiritual self.[8]

The practice of yoga offered Gautama high moral training that empowered him to resist aggressive desires such as lying, stealing, indulging in drinking or drugs, and harming other living creatures. Such behaviors are prime instincts of surviving that can be avoided completely.[9]

Gautama and other practitioners also mastered physical demands and learned to control their bodies in the face of basic physiological reactions, such as the heat and cold, or hunger and thirst. They practiced yoga by sitting still with no movement for hours so they could develop total control of their minds and bodies. Only when they demonstrated self-control and achieved a clear mental state were they allowed to advance to the next level of practice.[10]

When Gautama achieved physical and behavioral control, he began to practice advanced yoga, asana, which focused on a mental concentration, *Ekagrata*. This practice focuses the mind on a single point in order to observe the spiritual reflection of the soul.

After a long period of practice, Gautama eventually reached the trance level, *Jhana*. During trance he was unaware of external events; he could block all subjective thoughts and see himself objectively. This was the direct knowledge Alara had promised, when the ego and the illusions were no longer obstacles.[11] From *Jhana*, Gautama progressed to the highest level of meditation, known as "nothingness."

He indeed experienced success in mastering the *Dharma* teaching. But Gautama was not satisfied with the results because the trance experience did not provide long-lasting control over desire and ego.[12]

In the Sangha, Gautama learned skills that would assist him in the future, but he didn't feel that he belonged there, even though his teacher, Alara, offered him a position as teacher. Gautama continued to listen to his inner voice, which whispered to him to continue his search. He still had more to learn and experience. Gautama wished to find an everlasting peace resulted from a complete transformation.

Gautama mastered the art of reading signs. I am not referring to a "magic sign" given by a higher power, but rather road signs, just like the ones we see while we are driving. Some signs say "move on," like the sign that appeared in Gautama's life when he left his teacher. Some signs say, "change direction," such as when the current situation did not serve him anymore. Gautama's wanderings led him to a different Sangha, led by Uddaka Ramaputtaa, where he practiced, more or less, the same thing. But, different teachings brought him no closer to everlasting peace.[13]

Gautama was mentored by his teachers, and he certainly learned valuable skills, such as yoga and meditation. He was inspired to ask important questions that stimulated his intention of seeking enlightenment. Yet, Gautama realized that no matter how qualified the teacher was, the answers would not be found externally through knowledge, but through an internal process of "self" discovery. He could be his own teacher simply because the knowledge that he was seeking was already within; however, he needed to learn to access this information, which still remained a mystery. At this point Gautama left the Sangha, continuing to wonder and wander.

Step 3: Sources of Inspiration

Moses:
Moses Inspired to Seek Justice

Moses left Egypt as a result of his disappointment in Pharaoh's regime. Moses felt that he did not belong in his birth surroundings, since he didn't accept the way of life there and had no common ground with his fellow Egyptians. His actions to fight discrimination and make peace between people were constant evidence of his inner truth to promote justice in spite of the pervading societal attitude of discrimination.

When Moses acted on instinct, protecting the seven girls and their flock at the well, he did not know this would be a turning point in his direction. When the girls returned home, they told their father that Moses had helped them. The father was so impressed by the kindness of this Egyptian stranger that he invited Moses to the house.[14]

Jethro, the father of the seven daughters, happened to be the high priest and a spiritual leader of the tribe in Midian, who possessed outstanding moral values and leadership ability. He was the person to whom others in the community came to seeking advice, he was the one who resolved social situations in case of disagreement, and he was the mediator of communication between people. Jethro recognized similar qualities in Moses, and when the two men met, they felt an immediate soul connection.

Moses accepted Jethro's invitation to stay in Midian. Soon he married Jethro's daughter, Zipporah, and he took charge of Jethro's flock to contribute to the family's upkeep.[15]

This was a new chapter in Moses' life, which manifested exactly what he had wished for. Moses' journey into the "forest" of the unknown led him to stay in Midian, observing the leadership of his father-in-law.

Midian was not a big empire like Egypt, but a small tribe founded on a league of families as a supportive unit. All people had the same rights, and people were taught to respect and help one another. However, life in Midian was not perfect; people argued and disagreed as in any other community, but Jethro was able to mediate and maintain a normally functioning society.

The Bible doesn't say much about Moses' life in Midian, but we understand that he fit in almost immediately since he was part of the leading family, and both his wife and his father-in-law helped him to quickly learn what he needed to know. Moses had to learn about a cultural mindset that was quite different from the one he knew in Egypt.

In Midian, Moses learned how it was possible to live in harmony and peace and maintain a functional community in spite of the fact that people do disagree and fight for their own interest. Moses became Jethro's right hand, which gave him the unique position of being able to observe how his father-in-law managed his duties. He saw how his father-in-law mediated arguments and solved problems, how he judged people's misconducts, how he advised people and offered resolutions. All of this gave Moses great insight into how to achieve a better life through justice and service, and how to maintain harmony in the tribe.[16]

Moses noticed how his father-in-law saw his role of leadership as service to his community, whereas in Egypt the leader used people to serve his own wishes. This refreshing difference was a huge breakthrough that helped Moses to define his own passion. Moses, too, wanted to be a leader who established harmony and a peaceful life for his people.

Moses contemplated all that he was learning in Midian. He soon arrived at the conclusion that it was not enough to solve a problem when it comes.

There must be a way to prevent it from happening, he thought.

Watching the same situations recur over and over again, he realized that setting ground rules or defining codes of social conduct would prevent the problem from arising in the first place. That was the solution of law.

It is reasonable to assume that Moses was aware of the existence of law as a royal member. Yet, the law in Egypt was established by the king for his people. The king was not obligated to follow the law; he used the law to do as he wished. In Midian, Moses realized that laws should serve all people's needs and protect their rights.

Moses had developed his own original ideas, since justice was truly his passion and gift. But he didn't use his knowledge and his leadership abilities in Midian. He didn't have a purpose there, other than being a husband and a father. He could be a husband and father anywhere, but he couldn't be a leader where he was not needed. The tribe of Midian did not need Moses, but the poor slaves in Egypt could certainly use his help. Now he had a better idea of how to help them; he had the confidence and the passion that he had lacked before.

Living on the edge in two different places was the key for Moses' awakening. As with Buddha, Moses compared the two different lives he had and realized what was missing from his old life in Egypt. Changing the concept of law would help establish clear boundaries that would protect human rights and teach people to behave in a respectful way.

If only he could change the law, he thought.

Everything starts from a seed of thought, and Moses' mission was no exception. The idea of laws started to formulate in Moses' mind, and as it did, it was already in the making—since we now know that was Moses' contribution to the world.

Moses continued to think about the solution of law, but the truth was that he was a happy man and life in Midian was good. He was happily married with a family with strong connections, wealth, and peace of mind. Nothing was missing from his life except that he was not fulfilling his calling as a leader of justice. Moses finally understood that he needed to go back to Egypt to fulfill his passion and help those who truly needed it. (I will later explain Moses' decision in more depth.) Yet, Moses didn't plan to leave Midian for good. Later on, Moses brought the Israelites to the desert that he knew very well and settled near Midian, close to his tribal family.[17]

Jethro continued to mentor Moses in the desert of Midian, while leading the Israelites to freedom. Later on, the Bible tells us that Jethro observed Moses at work and provided his honest opinion to improve his performance as a leader. In one incident, Moses was overwhelmed by the Israelites' demands. He stayed out many hours to listen and help each person, but he was exhausted and incapable of doing it all by himself: "Moses sat as magistrate among the people, while the people stood about Moses from morning until evening."[18]

Jethro saw how much Moses was trying to do and knew he had to intervene. "But Moses' father-in-law said to him, 'The thing you are doing is not right; you will surely wear yourself out and these people as well.'"[19]

Jethro advised Moses to find a productive way to address the problems that Moses was trying to resolve. One of Jethro's suggestions was to delegate responsibility by creating a leadership team, leaving Moses available to make important decisions. "You shall seek out from among all the people capable men …trustworthy men…set these over them as chiefs of thousands.…Let them judge the people at all times. Have them bring every major dispute to you, but let them decide every minor dispute themselves."[20]

The mentoring relationship that Moses had with his father-in-law lasted throughout his lifetime.

Step 3: Sources of Inspiration

Jesus:
Jesus Inspired to Seek Compassion and Forgiveness

John the Baptist stood in the intersection of the Jezreel valley and the Jordan River during the High Holidays in the fall in order to get the attention of many people.[21]

Jesus joined the gathering crowd to listen to John the Baptist, the prophet from the Jordan Valley, who advocated repentance and baptized sinners in the Jordan River to purify their souls.[22]

Even though the Scripture does not explain the circumstances of this custom, it is reasonable to assume that this was the Jewish custom of "Tashlich," casting off the sin, which took place every year during the ten days of repentance between Rosh Hashana and Yom Kippur. During the ceremony of Tashlich, people throw pieces of bread as a symbol of all their sins into the river. I am inclined to believe that John baptized the people in the river to purify their souls and repent their actions from the previous year before Yom Kippur, which is a day of atonement when God would decide on their fate in the upcoming year.

Another explanation for the custom of Baptism can be found in the assumption that John belonged to the sect of Essenes who engaged in the ritual of bathing.[23]

John was born in the year 5 BCE in Jerusalem, in the village of Ein Kerem. Later on in life John left Jerusalem and went to the desert of Judea, where he joined the sect of the Essenes in the cave of Qumran.[24]

This sect prepared the way for the coming of a new Messiah through rituals. The historian, Josephus, said that the Essenes preformed rituals of Immersion and purification daily. They strongly believed the Bible prophecies, especially "Seventy Weeks Prophecy" in the book of Daniel about the time of the end, which fit the time of fulfillment as it mentioned in the Dead Sea Scroll, written by the Essenes' community.[25]

The Essenes believed in the coming of the Messiah, the "Teacher of all righteousness" who would establish the "New Convent" group of followers and fight against the corruption and moral decline among the Jewish community. The timing was just right for the upcoming Messiah.

John, as a passionate Essene, promoted this message, which eventually manifested through Jesus.

John's message attracted many followers who sought his knowledge and services. John welcomed people who wished to be baptized, but he explained to them clearly that the symbolic act of cleansing is not enough. "Repent; for the kingdom of Heaven is upon you!" he said.[26]

The task of purification does not end with an immersion in the river but requires acts of penitence, which grow out of compassion. John the Baptist encouraged people to change, to "clean up their act." They needed to address the situation, he said, and show real remorse and genuine intention to change and be better human beings.

John hoped to teach people the values of kindness and giving beyond the written law to create a significant change.

"So the crowds were asking him, "What then should we do?" John answered them, "The person who has two tunics must share with the person who has none, and the person who has food must do likewise."[27]

John's speech left an impression on young Jesus, who took John's words to heart.

According to the Scripture, right after Jesus was baptized, heaven's doors opened: "He saw the spirit of God descending like a dove to alight upon him…"[28]

Jesus was led by the Holy Spirit that appeared before him from the wilderness, where he fasted and went through a spiritual process of reflection for forty days. At this point, I am not going to discuss the conflict with the devil (which I will do later on), but I will focus on the fact that Jesus had forty days to think about the message he heard from John.

Jesus was inspired by John's message to think about significant change. He couldn't go back home and conduct a normal life after realizing the impact of this message. Jesus understood now that improving the quality of life does not depend on God's miracle as a reward for good behavior. Real change comes from the human effort to improve lives through acts of compassion. This idea led Jesus to a revolutionary approach, which stemmed from true love toward fellow man. He began to think about a social reform that would change the foundation of the Jewish law.

Jesus discovered that Jewish laws strives for fairness through justice, but lacked the compassion that would make people more sensitive to one another's needs. For example, the Jewish law wishes to establish a fair deal based on common sense, such as giving a loan plus interest to help a person in need;[29] yet, a person in need would have a hard time paying back the loan and the interest, which is a heavier load than he could carry. Besides, the interest on a loan gives the lender a chance to use the needy person in order to make a profit. Therefore, Jesus suggested the policy of the extra mile, which said that the stronger person should give more than the needy person needs in order to be compassionate towards the weak which truly need the help.

"If a man in authority makes you go one mile, go with him two."[30]

"If a man wants to sue you for your shirt, let him have your coat as well."[31]

Jesus believed that compassion should be the inner motive for actions, not the law's requirements.

Jesus was inspired to think about the virtues of compassion when he met John the Baptist, who had further instilled in him the principle of compassion. Although the timeline is not certain, it is possible that he was one of John's disciples being mentored by his teacher during the "missing" years, from the fall of 26 to the fall of 27 BCE. During this time, Jesus and John may have planned their vision and started a movement of revolution.[32]

According to the book *The Jesus Dynasty*, Jesus and John knew each other very well through the connection of their families. They spent time in Jerusalem with their families during the festivals, and they would visit each other in their respective hometowns.[33] No doubt it was these early family bonds that led to Jesus and John eventually planning a religious and political revolution that would put an end to the Roman rule in Judea, and would establish the foundation of the Kingdom of God.

Herod Antipas, son of Herod the Great and governor of Galilee, feared any kind of political resistance that would jeopardize his position as a leader and was especially wary of John the Baptist. John attracted many followers, and by late 27 BCE, the Jewish population seemed evenly divided between his supporters and those favoring Roman governance. Eventually, John's popularity led to his being arrested by the Romans.[34]

After John was taken by the Romans, Jesus felt responsible to carry on John's legacy. Jesus further developed John's concept to the point of changing the foundation of the Jewish law on the principles of love and compassion.

After Jesus' stay in the wilderness, he returned to Galilee determined to start his mission, regardless of the resistance he would face. Jesus knew that if he continued to carry John's message in public, he would be inviting the Romans to chase after him as well, and so he hid in Galilee to protect himself.[35]

Jesus hoped to change social norms simply by replacing the old foundation for justice with his new approach of using love and compassion. He knew that the kingdom of Heaven is not created by waiting for the Messiah to come; it is formulated in the here and now through people's actions. I believe Jesus was a visionary, who could see utopia, and his vision was unusual in his time. He hoped that each person willing to embrace these changes would be contributing to the collective effort of creating a Heaven on Earth: "You cannot tell by observation when the kingdom of God comes. There will be no saying, 'Look, here it is!' or 'There it is!'; for in fact, the kingdom of God is among you."[36]

Jesus didn't speak about Heaven as a future destination. Heaven is a description of ideal life on Earth that could be established through the human effort to change and improve life. I believe that Jesus understood the global impact that was caused by a change in mindset, he thought:

If everyone can live by the ideal of love and compassion, we will live in Heaven, he thought.

Jesus was undoubtedly inspired by the message he heard from John, of *how* to make the desirable change. He already possessed this desire but hearing it from John gave him the confirmation he needed to speak His truth. Jesus continued to develop the concept of the kingdoms of God through his own actions of resistance, modeling a new style of living.

Step 3: Sources of Inspiration

Muhammad:
Muhammad Inspired to Search for Balance

The Quraysh, the tribe Muhammad belonged to, was a very successful tribe in the seventh century; they had a monopoly on the main roads that led to major cities in Arabia. The accumulation of wealth gave the Quraysh a position of power, however, not all of that power was good. It increased the power of the greedy members who only wished to become richer and ignored their obligations to take care of the weaker families in the tribe.[37]

This caused a great deal of tension between families, as the rich became powerful and the poor struggled to make a living. Muhammad always paid attention to people in need; he saw what other people wished to ignore. Muhammad did not object to or disgrace people's efforts to make money and get rich; he himself was a man of means. However, Muhammad claimed that people should care for the collective. He thought it was not fair for one person to have a luxurious life and others hardly making a living. Muhammad did not accept the unjust lifestyle that had become the norm, and he used all of his personal resources to help people in need in times of crisis.

Muhammad spent many days by himself when he traveled the road, thinking about his desire to fix the social and economic inequity. As an independent thinker, he was an unusual man for his time, which distinguished him from the collective mindset and enabled him to follow his passion to make a difference.

Muhammad was inspired by monotheistic principles when searching for a solution for the social injustice between the poor and the rich. He thought about God's loving intention to give everyone a fair chance to live comfortably without worries.[38] He become familiar with monotheistic faith through his interaction with travelers on the road, such as Jewish tribes and Christian business people.[39] It make sense to him that the higher God, Al Llah, was the only ruler and creator of the world.

Muhammad always believed in Al Llah as not just the higher God, but the one and only God that created everything with perfect order and balance. He believed that God has all the power to control the world and provide stability and balance to all people.

If people would respect His will and live by His order they would help God to restore the world into its authentic order, he thought.

It is the people's responsibility to maintain this balance by following God's rules.

Muhammad met a few people who brought the monotheistic faith to his attention. These people exposed Muhammad to the central logic through the belief in one God that is established by monotheism. Muhammad was inspired by these people to think that the concept of monotheism could establish the change he hoped for.

Unlike Jesus, who was inspired by John the Baptist, Muhammad did not have a dominant mentor. He did, however, meet a few individuals who stimulated his awareness of the monotheistic belief and lifestyle. The first was a merchant from the Quraysh tribe, who converted to Christianity and hoped for a leadership position in the tribe in exchange for business ties with Byzantium. Later on, Muhammad's cousin and his wife's cousin converted to Christianity. They supported Muhammad during the period of his revelation and helped him understand his mission.[40]

It is my conclusion that Muhammad learned about the concept of God's law, which enforced the faith in one God from Judaism. It makes sense to him that the law is the manifestation of God's wish, which fits his true belief in Al Llah. If people will fulfill God' wish, God will restore his power to spread his resources equally between all people.

Muhammad didn't copy the same laws from Judaism since his focus was on financial order and not so much on the high morals emphasized by Moses' truth. Muhammad wished to focus on the financial justice that leads to peace of mind, according to the laws of the universe, as God intended. In that sense Muhammad's new revelation had original meaning.

Muhammad arrived at the conclusion that God's central sovereignty could only be enforced by law. This concept could unite the Arabian tribes of the Hijaz under Al Llah faith. Even though the Arabian tribes believed in the same Gods—Al Llah, the higher God, al-Lat, and al-Uzzah—and they performed the religious rituals in Mecca, each tribe had its own tradition. Their common faith did not unite the Arabian tribes who often fought against each other, caught in a cycle of revenge. Faith in Al Llah would change the cycle; the concept of a higher law as a manifestation of God's wish was a powerful tool of transformation.[41]

Up until that time, the Arabian tribes didn't have laws; instead they honored the custom of the Muruwah, a brotherhood bond to defend the members of the tribe against the enemy tribes. Muhammad was the first person to acknowledge the powerful implication of higher law to establish such a union.[42]

Later on, Muhammad established the Islam laws, which came to him directly from God through the revelation events.[43] The first thing he told his followers was to surrender to God's power. In fact, the word Islam means "submission." And by submission, Muhammad meant that God is the creator who created the world in perfect order, and people must obey God's laws in order to maintain this perfect balance. If people are greedy and selfish, they undermine God's work: they break the law of the Universe, which is a serious violation of divine order. If they are generous and kind, they help maintain God's order as He had planned it. Therefore, Muhammad believed in the power of law, which defined God's vision. "Goodness does not consist in turning your face toward East or West. The truly good are those who believe in God and the last day, in the angels, the Scriptures and the prophets; who gives away some of their wealth, however much they cherish it, to their relatives, to orphans, the needy, travelers and beggars, and to liberate those in bondage; those who keep up the prayer and pay the prescribed alms; who keep pledge whenever they make them; who are steadfast in misfortune, adversity and time of danger..."[44]

Muhammad developed a socialistic teaching, which reflected God's wish. Muhammad formed two options. The first was obligated duty, which he called *zakat*, meaning that every person must give a portion of his income to offer financial support for the weak. Everyone is responsible for maintaining a normal balance among all people in the community.[45]

In addition, Muhammad offered a second option of charity, which would give people credit for their generosity. These credits would be reported in the court of God, where people would be judged for success or failure to fulfill God's wish.

Muhammad planned to establish an idealistic community based on financial balance to create the everlasting harmony as it is found in Heaven.

"... and their Lord gives them the good news of His mercy and pleasure, Gardens where they will have lasting bliss..."[46]

The Spiritual Lesson of Inspiration

Walking in the "forest" is a very challenging and frightening task, and yet the Universe is providing us with "direction signs" connecting us with people that will show us the way and help us discover the option that our soul is craving.

The Universe is behind us, guiding our path. If we need a familiar soul to feel safe in the beginning of the unknown journey, the Universe will provide it. If we need to stop and rethink our direction, the Universe will support it. If we need to take a different turn and explorer another possibility, the Universe will show it to us. Whatever makes us feel safe and whatever feels right for us is being delivered to us. The flow of changes in our lives is depending on our level of openness to allow it. Let me illustrate by example.

A short time after arriving to the United States in 1999, I was making a living from teaching Judaic studies at a Jewish private school. It was natural for me to link into the Jewish community, holding on to familiar tradition. It also felt safe to rely on help from my Jewish–Israeli co-workers while I was making my first adjustment into the multi-cultural country. I wasn't seeking my truth at this point, but I had to learn how to survive in the "forest," as the rules of function in a new country had changed. For instance, I had to learn how to speak a different language; I had to adjust to the long hours at work and the two day weekends, compared to the short hours at work during six days of working a week in Israel; I had to adjust to many different customs that were very strange to me at first.

The first three months I lived in a temporary place, but when I was searching for a permanent place, I felt in my heart that I needed to be in a neutral environment, one far away from the school community or the Israeli community. By doing this, I was hoping to blend in and feel the impact of living in a strange country. Living in a non-Jewish environment set my intention to interact with the non-Jews around me, but I wasn't ready to seek a real opportunity to interact as long as I depended on the Jewish community for help. And yet something had changed throughout the years as I started to attract experiences that showed me the direction of my heart.

The first person who came into my life was my real estate agent who invited me to Christmas dinner. During the same year I met my boyfriend, a Muslim from Iran who mirrored me in what was holding me back. The last person, against all odds, was a Palestinian friend. All these people showed me different options that I was craving to discover. Yet, it took me a few years before I felt safe enough to remove the social barriers and engage my life fully with the essence of oneness that I was seeking ever since I was six years old.

As we noticed from the Masters' journeys, the messages they heard from mentors and people that crossed their path were the road maps for their destinations. The messages we receive from people we meet show us other options, which are the direction of our hearts. These kinds of messages are not just signs of where to go next, but they are transformational clues that help us see our desired destination.

The Universe helps us feel safe while walking in the "forest," and yet, it points us slowly and continuously to the direction of our hearts. We have to be clear on our intention and pay attention to the signs the show up in our lives. When we honor our truth, we are going in the right direction, which is right for us. When we walk against it, we face conflicts and crises that lead to a "dead-end." Listening to our inner voice keeps us on our journey and helps us find our destination.

Just as when we travel to a strange country, we look at a road map and pay attention to signs because we wish to be aware of the "direction signs" as we are traveling through the journey of life.

A starter to implement the teaching of source of inspiration:
- Identify the forest you have to enter.
- Pay attention to the people that hold an arrow sign, showing you a new possibility and a new direction.
- Ask yourself what makes more sense to you.
- Be open to hear messages as they show up in your life. Their timing is divine intervention ready to make a change.

PART II

INTERNAL PROCESS OF TRANSFORMATION

Transformation literally means going beyond your form.
~Wayne Dyer

CHAPTER 4

REPROGRAMMING: THE DEATH OF THE OLD SELF

You cannot solve a problem with the same mind that creates it.
~Albert Einstein

Our spiritual quest starts when we leave home, cutting the link to the given truth presented by the norm to go on an independent journey. We finally venture out of the house, learning new things, experiencing a new style of living, and being exposed to different beliefs that expand our horizons.

At the beginning of this journey, we observe new information with curiosity, open to learn and adjust to the new life as outsiders. When we adjust to the new life, we become participators, taking an active role in the new surroundings.

This change of lifestyle is the beginning of the internal process of transformation, as we adapt to a new mindset. The transition happens naturally, but we may be reluctant to accept it, trying hard to hold on to the old and familiar. Most of us have a hard time letting go of old beliefs because they are such a strong foundation of our identity. In letting go of old values, we are losing our identity.

The hardest part of this process is to distance ourselves from the people we love from the past who are still holding onto the same values that we wish to liberate from. We don't want to lose the people we love just because we are no longer agreeing on the same values. In fact, our wish to be loved and accepted by them is bigger than our desire to live by the values that make much more sense to us. And so, we often compromise on our own truth just to be part of the tribe and feel a sense of belonging.

In some cases, the environment we need to disconnect from is emotionally toxic for us, and if we choose to hold on to it, we would get sucked into the drama or continue to embrace the same habit that isn't good for us. The negative influences of our environment will control our feelings and choices to keep us stuck. Therefore, distance and separation from unhealthy situations will help us to walk toward change and step away from anything that doesn't serve us.

As a result of cutting the cord to the past, we find ourselves grieving the loss of our old life, paradoxically resisting the newness and simultaneously embracing it. If we continue to resist change, we will be unable to create our desired life.

The process of grieving—known as "The Judgment Day" in the Scriptures—is referring to a day that will put an end to the old order. In the Scriptures, the Judgment Day refers to a day of destruction and universal war that leads to a complete transformation—but the Judgment Day is really a metaphor for an inner struggle, which is an individual process of Judgment. We are judging ourselves, realizing that our old life is coming to an end. The past is gone, the present feels like discontent, and the future is unknown. In the new world, we are not the same as we once were, but the new "self" has not yet fully formulated.

The shift into the new life happens through a process of reprogramming our thoughts and changing of values. By letting go of the old thinking pattern and values, we are making room for a new way of life. The Masters did exactly that when they gave up on their old values and beliefs that caused chaos, crisis, and were insufficient in resolving new circumstances. The Masters were able to shift their thinking and create alternative values that would replace the old and the broken beliefs. Yet, they had to go through their own "dark night of the soul" process to give themselves the permission to move forward. They had to deal with grief and sadness, realizing that there was a price for walking away from their tribe's values.

In this chapter, I will describe first the individual struggle of each of the Masters to cut the cord from the old mindset, which involves an internal process of grieving. They all had to acknowledge that the old values didn't work and that they should follow their own truth, but in order to do this, they had to overcome their personal grieving.

Step 4: Reprogramming

Buddha:
Buddha's Near-Death Experience

Gautama lived in the forest as a "homeless" to pursue the course of a holy man. He experienced the suffering that stemmed from the struggle to survive in rough surroundings:

"I can recall, Sariputta, how I practiced the four-square practice of the holy life. Thus, I was penance-worker, outdoing others in penance. I was a rough-liver, outdoing others in roughing it…I went without cloth, I licked my food from my hands…I lived on roots and fruits from the forest; on casual fruits (that had fallen) I existed…I was one who wore coarse clothes; I wore hemp woven in with other things, grave-cloths, dustheap rags…I was a thorn-bed man and lay upon a bed of thorn."[1]

Gautama eventually became accustomed to the life of a wandering hermit who struggled to survive in the forest.

After abandoning the Yogi and the Sangha, he thought about his next move. "Dwelling in the crowd is no good for discipline in practice of austerity; therefore, I will retain five disciples only,"[2] he said. They all went on a journey to Urubilva, the village of Senapati. Gautama found a grove of trees near the Nairañjanā River and sat there fasting.[3] They practiced ascetics in order to practice self-control and redeem bad karma. "And thus far did I go in roughing it. The dirt of many seasons gathered on my body just like the outer crust of the tree-bark."[4]

They believed that body torture, *tapas* (ascetic practice to achieve spiritual purification), would redeem karmic debt and would move them closer toward enlightenment; but in practice, body torture and fasting only increased the pain of suffering, leading to regression and not progression.[5]

At this point, Gautama's body was failing and was close to death: "In the end he grew so weak that he fell into a faint; and if companions had not been around to feed him some warm rice gruel, he could easily have died."[6] Having lost his strength, Gautama concluded that all his practice was useless. "No one engaged in the discipline of ascetic striving has ever transcended suffering; therefore, this path is not adequate for knowledge."[7]

Gautama began to take substantial food (porridge and gruel), rubbed his limbs with ghee and oil, and took a bath. Gradually he regained his strength and left.

All his life, Gautama was searching for the *Dharma* (searching for his true essence, a life path). The *Dharma* depends on the caste system that defines the normal behavior of its members. Gautama lived his life by the rules of the Hindu society, firstly as a prince. After he broke his commitment to the caste, he continued to be a "follower" as a holy man. At first, he observed the life of suffering from the point of view of a participant; then he practiced yoga and meditation and learned about the process of liberation. Gautama realized that his days in the Sangha came to an end because all his studying had not led to a breakthrough. Lastly, Gautama fasted with a group of monks to redeem bad karma. But as long as Gautama placed his fate in the hands of others, he did not reckon with his own *Dharma*.

He considered giving up and returning home.

Gautama went to the village of Senayani, where he was invited to stay by a man named Sena. Sena's two daughters knew the prince's true identity. They prepared rice-milk for Gautama exactly when he was determinate to stop his fasting.

The women's intervention with food is a well-known motif from the story of Paradise and the *Epic of Gilgamesh*, where the women used food as seduction. Both Eve and the harlot from the Gilgamesh stories were responsible for the men's transformations from simple states to more complex ones, preparing them for a new phase of life.

Gautama was no exception, since the girls facilitated his healing. He finished his meal and asked the girls, "What did you seek by virtue of your gift?"[8]

They replied, "We would like to have you as a husband, the prince of Sakyas, since the soothsayer predicted that you would become a Cakravartin King."[9]

Gautama replied, "This is not possible; I am the one who wandered forth and have no desire for sensual pleasure."[10] Gautama refused to go back to the normal life he used to have as a prince. He wished to be a free man without any obligation.

In another version of the story, the girls were Mara's daughters, whom he sent to test Gautama's intention to continue his journey in spite of his disappointment from the effort and time invested in it.

The fictional version of the story in Deepak Chopra's book, *Buddha: A Story of Enlightenment*, brought a much broader meaning to the meeting with Mara, who wished to undermine Gautama's progress.

At first, Mara appeared to Gautama saying that he could teach him what Gautama had failed to learn in the Sangha. "I know the secrets of the universe. No knowledge can be kept from me since my role is to see into crevices of every soul. I will share all that I know with you."[11]

Mara's appearance is very similar to the devil's temptation of Jesus, offering to give Him everything if He worships him. The connection between the two dialogues indicates a turning point in both Gautama's and Jesus' lives as they weighed their options between two choices: fulfilling material desires or spiritual callings.

Gautama answered Mara indifferently. "No, the one who wanted to know everything no longer exists."[12]

Mara, striving to divert Gautama's attention, sent his daughters over to swim in the river while he implored him to marry one of his daughters. Gautama answered again with indifference. "The man who once had a wife no longer exists."[13]

Gautama was confident that he no longer desired the pleasures of life. He realized for the first time that he was not the same person he used to be. He was no longer a proprietor carrying the obligation of his caste. He was no longer a "homeless" wandering among the hermit communities. That Gautama no longer existed. The only way he could move forward was by detaching from the past—to accept the change.

We notice that the process of grieving comes long after the actual act of walking away from the past. This happened to Moses who left Egypt and settled down in Midian, and many years later he faced the implication of his act. Buddha, too, left his family a long time ago, but now he realized that the direction he took was irreversible—there was no point in going back.

Gautama was at a crossroads. On one hand, he was disappointed in the life of austerities, which he practiced with all his effort, studying the two popular approaches introduced by his teachers. He was extremely disappointed from the fasting period, during which he was unable to achieve liberation. On the other hand, he was unable to consider the option of going back to be a "householder" again. Even if he considered going back home, he would not fit in. He was different from the person he was just a few years ago, and going back in time would not be possible.

Life must progress forward, but what direction should I go? he wondered.

Gautama sat down, crossed his legs, and determined: "I will not uncross my legs until the destruction of defilements has been attained"[14]

To overcome grieving, Gautama realized he had to detach from the past, accepting his new direction. When he was still a wandering hermit, prior to his Sangha experience, he recalled many moments of missing his loving family and being loved and cared for. He also missed his comfortable bed and warm bath. He was haunted by the feelings of guilt from abandoning his family and betraying his loving father who tried so hard to protect him. Gautama realized that his feelings were holding him back from moving on. He could not allow himself to be tortured by his thoughts since he had done nothing intentionally to hurt his family. He just wanted to go on his own journey and follow his own passion. Gautama understood that he couldn't go back. No doubt his family still loved him and would have been happy to have him back, but nothing would have been the same.

At this point, Gautama realized that he no longer wished to fulfill selfish desires such as family life, sex and pleasure, and fame through his position as a prince. He wished to continue along the path of a holy man and find a different way to achieve complete liberation.

Once again, Gautama used the principle of non-attachment to disengage from his learning experience, realizing that this knowledge no longer served him. Although he appreciated the experience, and he certainly used many of the skills he learned, he was no longer attached to a method of teaching that is good for all being. He wished to uncover the knowledge from within. Letting go of a concept that didn't work would make room for something new that might work.

The principle of non-attachment is intended to liberate a person from the residue of the past, which would influence his mind. Every person who lets go of an old mindset is on his way to creating a new and improved life.

Step 4: Reprogramming

Moses:
The Judgment Day from Moses' Point of View

After escaping from Egypt, Moses settled down in Midian where he found peace of mind.

For a couple of years, Moses took care of Jethro's flock. He enjoyed being a father and raising his family. His frequent visits to the desert, where he took the flock to eat, gave him a chance to relax and meditate.

In my imagination, each time Moses went to the desert, he closed his eyes to think about his life. At first, he was thinking about his loving wife and beloved son who brought him the greatest joy. He was pleased that he had a wonderful and supportive father-in-law. He belonged to the leading family in the tribe of Midian and enjoyed a prosperous life with money, popularity, and respect. Life couldn't have been better. Moses was grateful for a life that was completely opposite from his life in Egypt.

I believe that Moses continued to wander while visiting the remote desert—this time he wandered in thoughts about his life back in Egypt. As he looked at himself wearing his shepherd's clothes, he was shocked to realize that he was no longer an Egyptian. He had a new identity and a new lifestyle based on a new mindset. Nothing of his old life was relevant to his life in Midian.

Moses' life had changed so much since he left Egypt. He had gained the wisdom of living harmony and maintaining social functions from the life in Midian. He never had any conflict with the people in Midian or with the lifestyle he experienced there. The norm and the lifestyle in Midian suited his nature and made him feel at home.

He never felt that way in Egypt, where he was born. Even though Moses was culturally Egyptian, his resistance of the Egyptian way of life made him an outsider. Giving up on his old identity as an Egyptian was inevitable. Moses took time to reflect on it, for the first time since he left, in order to accept it. When he quieted his mind, he was able to see his own transformation, consumed by inner thoughts:

How can I be Egyptian if I don't look like one, but more importantly, if I don't behave or think the same way they do?

Sitting by himself in the desert gave Moses the chance to grieve his old self, going through the "dark night of the soul."

The first part of the process was knowing that he was never an Egyptian according to their standards. Even though he was loved by his relatives, and he had good memories as well as bad ones, he never felt he belonged there.

The second part was more complex since he understood that he would never again be part of his homeland. If Egypt wasn't home in the past, it wouldn't be home in the future. Moses had rejected once and for all his past identity and past life in Egypt in order to accept his life the way it was.

The change of consciousness that happened through a process of reprogramming could not happen in Moses' birth surroundings. The change happened in a neutral place where he was exposed to a different mindset, which was created by new experiences.

Moses' true self indicated the potential to fight for justice, but he was not fully aware of it while living in Egypt because justice was not a value the Egyptians honored. It was in Midian—and watching his father-in-law's just leadership—where Moses finally became aware of the true essence he wished to live by.

Could he be considered Midiani? Could he carry the Midianic identity for the rest of his life?

Before Moses could go on and choose his new identity, he had to be clear on his wish to disconnect from the Egyptian culture because neither the mindset nor the values he was brought up with would serve him in the present or in the future. Moses was going through the process of grieving the loss of his old identity so he could have closure. He knew from that point on that he was a new man.

The idea of letting go of the old beliefs as a collective effort to change lives is expressed through the religious concept of the "End of the Days" in Judaism. The prophet, Isaiah, claimed that the redeemer (i.e. the Messiah) would put an end to the old structure in order to create a new order that united all the nations. "Thus He will judge among the nations…and they shall beat their sword into plowshares and their spears into pruning hooks: nation shall not take up sword against nation; they shall never again know war."[15]

This symbolic meaning describes the process of "self" judgment when one is coming to the realization that one chapter in his or her life is over before opening a new one.

Moses faced his own "Judgment Day" as a process of "self" judgment, asking himself the question of where he truly belonged. From Moses' inspiration we learn that we belong where we truly feel harmony with the values and the lifestyle that make sense to us. Nothing else matters.

Whether or not "The Judgment Day" is an individual process or a collective effort to change, it is our responsibility to do the work that will allow us to accept the change and move on to the next chapter in our lives. The "redemption" act of building a new life and establishing new identity would not be possible without the process of destruction. Moses had to let go of his old identity and find peace with the ending of the old chapter.

Step 4: Reprogramming

Jesus:
The End of the Days through Jesus' Eyes

Jesus was an enthusiastic student who was fascinated by the essence of the Torah. He truly envisioned the ideal style of living that was established through the moral and the law of the Torah. Yet his proficiency in the Jewish law gave him the confidence to express his own views and point out the shortcomings of the *Halachah* (the Jewish law).

Jesus concluded that the Jewish laws were founded on the principle of fairness, such as, "An eye for eye and a tooth for a tooth," which only offered a minimal solution to a problem, was not enough to ensure that people would avoid harmful behavior.

Jesus had a better idea. He wished to change the foundation of the Jewish law to the concept of compassion, which is the opposite to the principle of justice.

Jesus believed that if people were motivated by compassion, they would be able to give and do good things without limitations. They would be sensitive to others' needs. "But you must love your enemies and do good; And lend without expecting any return."[16]

Jesus hoped to teach people the importance of loving your fellow man by doing something good without any gain. "When you are having a party for lunch or supper, do not invite your friends, your brothers… they will only ask you back again and so you will be repaid. But when you give a party, ask the poor, the crippled, the lame and the blind, and so find happiness."[17] People should open their hands with their heart.

On one occasion, Jesus was asked why his students were picking up corn on Shabbat. According to the Ten Commandments, performing an act of work on Shabbat is a crime against God. "You shall not do any work."[18]

Jesus defended his students:

"Have you not read what David did when he and his men were hungry? He went into the house of God and ate the sacred bread, though neither he nor his men had a right to eat it, but only the priests. Or have you not read in the law that on Shabbat the priests in the temple break the Shabbat and it is not held against them? I tell you, there is something greater than the temple here…"[19]

Jesus explained that being hungry was a good enough reason to break the law—even their beloved king of Israel committed this crime. They should understand the motive behind the crime before judging or condemning it.

Jesus did not accept the measurement of justice according to which people learn their lesson through punishment and fear. He described a brand new vision about the ideal life of hope and love. Jesus saw himself as a messenger of change, who had a plan to improve life. Eventually, Jesus announced his intention to change the Jewish law on the Sermon on the Mount. "Do not suppose that I have come to abolish the law and the prophets; I did not come to abolish, but to complete."[20]

By setting this intention, Jesus wished to uproot the old concept of justice and eliminate destructive behavior from its roots. Jesus hoped that getting rid of the old that didn't work would make room for something better to improve the quality of life.

Such a revolutionary idea has an impact on personal "grieving," which occurs normally when a person is replacing one mindset with another and changing lives.

When one stops thinking like everyone else, one is becoming an outsider. Though Jesus never claimed that he was an outsider among the Jews, he conducted a way of life that contradicted the Jewish lifestyle and broke many of the Jewish laws. He disconnected himself from the Jewish core simply by living up to his own truth. He had to pay the price for fighting for what he believed in.

It is reasonable to assume that Jesus had to experience the emotional process of "grieving" in his own life, considering the personal implications of walking away from the past. Yet, the Scriptures lack information about this. In fact, the Scriptures are missing many years from Jesus' life before starting his mission. Jesus took time off in the desert dealing with his feelings as we can sense from his dialogue with the devil (which I will discuss later on). During that time, Jesus acknowledged the fact that different times call for different measurements. When Jesus said, "I did not come to abolish, but to complete,"[21] he was telling people that the old system was no longer working, and it was time for a change. Jesus wished to make room for a new form of life, insisting on living his life according to the principles of love and compassion in order to pave the way for change.

Jesus taught his followers to give up on the old system that no longer functioned at its best. The End of the Days indicated a time to uproot the broken and rusty old foundation to make room for a new and improved style of living. "Behold! I am making all things new!"[22]

The new will take place only when the old is completely gone.

This cycle of destruction and reconstruction is an ongoing process throughout history. We have witnessed old social and political system collapse, such as the collapse of Communism in Russia, because they failed to accommodate the public's needs. After the First World War in 1922, Communism united people and gave them hope of rebuilding their lives by working together under the slogan, "Peace, Bread, and Land." It gave people a sense of stability and security that the government was looking after them. But in 1989, that was no longer the need. People discovered the beauty of freedom and the essence of individuality, which could not bloom in communistic surroundings.

The Book of Revelation emphasizes this principle by saying that fire will destroy the old as a final act, which will cleanse and purify the world. "For the old order has passed away."[23] The symbol of fire for total destruction indicates a normal phase of cleansing and letting go of the old values that no longer work within new circumstances and are no longer relevant. As long as we hold onto the old tradition, we are keeping our own progress on hold, preventing us from making room for something new and something better. By letting go, and putting the old behind, we will be able to move forward.

Step 4: Reprogramming

Muhammad:
Muhammad's Morning Brightness

While still in Mecca, Muhammad could not ignore the hardships of his close friends and relatives who struggled to provide for their families. He was disappointed to see tribe members dishonoring their commitment to the Muruwah custom, which agreed that members of the tribe would be held responsible for other members. Originally, this custom was an agreement to protect the members against other tribes. The members of the tribe had to defend their fellow tribesmen and obey the chief. Each had the duty to cultivate Muruwah to ensure that the tribe would survive.[24]

Muhammad became aware of the social tension between the families and tried his best to assist people he knew. He had hoped that the well-off members of the tribe would be helping out other members financially. But instead, a few families became richer and stronger, while the rest became poorer and weaker. Muhammad felt strongly that this mindset should be replaced in order to resolve the problem and avoid social destruction.

The new mindset that was influenced by monotheistic principles made much more sense. Muhammad knew that the belief in one God would create a strong foundation to establish change. If he could convince people to stop believing in other gods and give their faith to the one God, it would be possible to achieve the balance in all aspects of life. Muhammad simply was suggesting replacing one mindset with another.

For this to occur, everyone had to accept Al Llah first as the one and only God. With this acceptance, the world would be perceived as having one logic, one order, and one function, which would lead to the elimination of paganism in Arabia and would give Al Llah absolute control. [25]

The second change needed was to define God's wish through a higher law, which was a revolutionary idea in Arabia since every tribe had its own norm, and the only thing close to a law was the custom of Muruwah. Yet, the concept of law was necessary to enforce God's wish. If people would obey God's laws, they would be able to maintain the perfect balance and harmony that God had intended.

Muhammad himself believed in Al Llah as the only God, but he didn't have a clear vision. According to the written version, Muhammad's vision came to him one night while praying in a cave in Mount Hira—known as his revelation event. This was where he had a direct communication with God through the intervention of the angel Gabriel.[26]

Muhammad was shocked and frightened to discover his true calling. He realized that something in his life was about to change and he could no longer resist it, but he was scared.

Muhammad continued to receive messages from God each time he returned to the cave. After the first few revelation events, Muhammad was more confused than ever. In fact, he didn't tell anyone about it except his wife, Khadija, who tried to help him understand what it meant. She told him not to be afraid of his mission since he was already fulfilling God's wish. He was already kind and helping others to ease their burden and resolve their personal problems. Muhammad had started God's mission before he was assigned to it—and if God was truly giving him this mission, He would assist him in making it happen.[27]

But Muhammad's mission required a lot more than being kind and caring. Muhammad had to fight the old tradition that was honored by his relatives, friends, and the tribe members. He had to be sure that he was strong enough to walk away from the old and embrace the changes that his mission might bring.

Muhammad went through a period of silence that lasted two years, during which he tried to fathom the meaning of his revelation.[28] This time was a personal crisis as Muhammad came to realize that his old life as a tribesman was coming to an end. He could not live by the old mindset that led society to destruction.

The motif of a Judgment Day also indicates "self" judgment when Muhammad realized that it was time to destroy the old foundation before building a new one. But he himself had to go the same process of grieving his old life. I am inclined to believe that Muhammad had a hard time tearing the family apart and destroying the unity of the tribe's structure, which was already being destroyed by greed. Muhammad had to prepare himself for resistance even from his closest friends and relatives. Some people would even think that he was crazy. But above all, Muhammad had to give up the life he had known for the life in the "forest,"—for something vague and unclear—since his vision was not yet crystallized. He was passionate about making change, and he truly believed it was necessary, but he also had to weigh the practical impact of his move.

The Sura [93] in the Koran, "The Morning Brightness," is a reflection of Muhammad's own mourning before accepting his mission, a period that lasted two years following his first revelation. Only a few people whom he trusted knew about his mission. In this Sura, Muhammad showed the growth of belief in himself:

> "By the morning brightness, and by the night when it grows still
> Your Lord has not forsaken you (prophet) nor does He hate you.
> And the future will be better for you than the past
> Your Lord is sure to give you so much that you will be well satisfied.
> Did He not find you an orphan and shelter you?
> Did He not find you lost and guide you?
> Did He not find you in need and make you self-sufficient?
> So do not be harsh with the orphan
> And do not chide the one who asks for help.
> Talk about the blessing of your Lord."[29]

Muhammad's "dark night of the soul" is expressed through this poem, dealing with two different issues. Firstly, uprooting the old, which causes resistance to rebuild something else to replace it. Muhammad acknowledged that the old system did not function, and the new direction of wealth only caused more problems. Secondly, Muhammad had confidence in God's power to bring balance and harmony, but he didn't have a plan. He didn't know how everything would fall into place. How could he reveal his vision to the public if he didn't quite have a vision? He had to trust God to deliver the answers when the time was right.

Khadija was a supportive wife; she saw Muhammad's pain and confusion after the first revelation and suggested that Muhammad consult with her cousin, Waraqa who studied the Scriptures and could give him expert advice. Waraqa had no doubt at all; he immediately recognized the prophet and cried, "Holy! Holy! he cries at once: If you have spoken the truth to me, O Khadija, there has come to him the greatest *namus* who came to Moses aforetime, and lo, he is the prophet of this people."[30]

Waraqa took Muhammad to the Ka'abe where a group of Christians welcomed the new prophet with kisses on his forehead.[31] That marked the first time Muhammad received public recognition as a prophet.

Muhammad slowly gained the trust and the confidence to believe in his mission. His first step was to demolish the old pagan tradition. Muhammad explained to his believers that God did not bring harmony by himself, but through believers who were responsible for fulfilling God's plan. Each person is responsible for doing his or her part by obeying God's laws and fulfilling His plan.

Muhammad dedicated his life's mission to establishing the principles of Islam and bringing a radical change to Arabia.

The Spiritual Lesson of Reprogramming

The process of transformation starts when we first acknowledge the core value we wish to live by. The shift of consciousness is already taking place, but we are not able to grasp it yet because we need time to digest the changes and accept the new mindset. At this point, our life seems to be on hold. Nothing external may have happened, but our inside world turns upside down.

I personally suffered from depression while working in an Orthodox Jewish school—feeling trapped inside the Jewish walls and unable to honor my truth of interacting with the non-Jewish world.

In 2005, I finally left the school and moved into a cottage house so I could be alone. I sat in my house for months, grieving my old life because deep down, I knew that my Jewish life had come to an end. I didn't have any friends to talk to; I didn't have any job to go to; and I didn't have any life routine. My life was standing still.

Giving up on my Jewish life was a difficult process but going back to it was not an option. If I had done so, I would have continued to be trapped in the same situations as before. I wanted to start to live my life again, but I had to take time to heal before I figured out what my new identity would be. I was a woman living on the edge without a certain future.

Until we know who we truly are, the universe will not know how to guide us. Most people are stuck between the past and the future, just like a ghost. They are moving to new surroundings, but they are still holding on to the old way of thinking that keeps them mentally stuck. This is similar to immigrants who move to a new country, but they still live among themselves to preserve the old mindset. Being a "ghost," getting stuck between two states, is not an option. If we wish to create a better future, we must be ready to let go of the old values that are no longer serving us.

Letting go of the past requires detachment and emotional grieving, which also involves isolation and quiet time as we noticed from the Masters' journeys. This quiet time appears in many different ways in our life; sometimes even in the form of a long-term illness that forces us to take time out from our usual routines. This break is only a turning point in our lives that leads us in a new direction—if we take the time to do the work.

In spite of the challenge to lose our old lives, we have a potential to discover a new sense of freedom to live by our truth. More so, when we change, we are paving the path of change, modeling a new way of life that will improve life as a whole.

Every person who is capable of letting go of the past has the power to change and progress society. Human history teaches us that we are in a constant process of evolution. The future is a continuation of the present, and the present is a continuation of the past. Therefore, redemption is a natural process of improvement that depends on an "omnipotent man," who has the ability to create a better tomorrow. Thus, it is human beings, who through their own abilities and skills, will redeem humanity from its suffering.

A starter to implement the teaching of reprogramming:
- Identify what mindset and values are no longer relevant to your life at the present.
- Take the time to replace the old values that keep you stuck with the new values that you wish to live by.
- Eliminate what you don't accept so you can get closer to your truth.

CHAPTER 5

EPIPHANY: AN INNER DIALOGUE WITH OUR HIGHER SELF

The cave you fear to enter holds the treasure you seek.
~ Joseph Campbell

During the grieving time, we tend to withdraw from the crowd and be in isolation. It is not our emotional state that compels us to do so, but our need for quiet time. We want to go to a quiet place without noise that overshadows our own inner voice. In a place where we are surrounded by people, we tend to listen to other people's voices. We tend to follow the social expectations and ignore our own voice, if we can even hear it.

We need time off every once in a while to silence the mind, which many people achieve through meditation. Meditation has a similar effect as going to a quiet place, yet we need to develop our listening skills gradually so we can become accustomed to hearing our own voice. This way we can trust our own intuition to determine what is right for us.

When I studied the life journey of the Masters, I noticed that Jesus, Muhammad, Moses, and Buddha took time off to be by themselves in order to connect internally with their higher self. They took the time to disconnect from their busy and commonplace lives in order to think about their life's purpose. They had to satisfy their existing needs as humans, but they felt that material accomplishments were not enough to sustain their souls, which craved so much more. According to the Scriptures, the resulting higher level of communication they achieved was expressed through the intervention of God's messenger.

Even though we are not approached by an angel the same way they were, we too take the time to reflect on our life's directions and find our own happiness. Normally, the self-reflection period in our lives happens in midlife, during which we feel the need to shift priority in order to live a meaningful life. We, too, are going through inner conflicts in order to address fears and concerns that are holding us in place. We tend to worry about how we are able to make it happen and how to keep balance. But when we weigh our options, we could find the solution to overcome the obstacles. As we examine the Masters' dialogue, we become aware of this process.

The dialogues that the Masters experienced with a higher entity continued for a long period before they were able to make the decision to move forward and live up to their true calling. The inner communication happened when they were by themselves in a place far away from human interaction so they could truly rethink their life's purpose. Jesus stayed in the desert for forty days during which he had a dialogue with the devil; Buddha sat under the Bodhi tree for forty-nine days communicating with Mara (a devilish creature); Moses most likely went to the desert every day, meeting the Angel of God behind the burning bush; and Muhammad spent many nights in the cave in Mount Hira communicating with Angel Gabriel. The communication through the messenger of God is a form of inner communication with their higher "self"— conflicting between their need to survive, accomplishing egoistic goals, and carrying a public mission for the sake of serving other human beings. Both the angels and the devil were facilitating inner communication, intending to challenge them and test their intention so they will be ready to rise above basic subsistence and take on a journey of purpose.

To some, this conflict sounds familiar. It isn't easy to rethink our life's direction; we have so much to consider and so many risks to take. This form of inner communication is helping us to reevaluate life.

We all need time out from our busy routines and to ask ourselves the most important questions:

Am I pleased with my accomplishments? What am I still hungry for?

We all go through this phase of life one way or another. In fact, this is the midlife crisis, which usually happens around the age of forty. Up until then, we did everything to establish our existence. We built our career and reputation, made money and bought a house, created a family, and built a strong foundation to live a functional life. But those are not the only things we wish to accomplish in our lifetime. We want to make an impact and leave our legacy.

In this chapter, I will continue to demonstrate how each Master dealt with this same dilemma throughout a long stagnant period through which he evaluated his life's purpose. The self-reflection events accrued in their lives resulted with epiphanies, preparing each of them to make a life-changing decision.

Step 5: Epiphany

Buddha:
Paving the Middle Way

G autama had been gone from his home for a long time. His first act of going forth was carefully considered through an inner conflict with Mara, the ruler of the Universe.

Mara was a fictional character similar to a demonic creature, which challenged Gautama to go back to a normal life, to live by the social expectations defined by the caste system of the Hindu tradition. This tempting proposal recurred many times even though Gautama had already taken the first step toward transforming his life according to the spiritual dictates of his inner calling.

Gautama was unclear about his future, but he knew that he was not going back to the life of a householder—that chapter was long gone, and he must continue what he started. But Mara kept appearing every time Gautama had doubt and hesitation about his journey.

After years of study and intense spiritual practice in the Sangha, Gautama decided to continue his journey alone. He sat in an uncomfortable position and strived to focus his efforts on attaining enlightenment. Mara appeared before him again—this time mounted on an elephant and accompanied by his army.[1]

Mara was taking advantage of Gautama's vulnerability, sending nine storms toward him to intimidate him, but the strength of the storms did not deflect Gautama from his mission. Gautama was well-aware of Mara's attempt to challenge him and had convinced himself to ignore his presence.

Mara should not undermine my intention to pursue spiritual life, he repeated this thought:

Undeterred, Mara next tried to distract Gautama with a verbal confrontation that demanded a response:

"Rise up, Siddhartha, warrior prince afraid of death, how dare you seat yourself in my seat. You have ventured where you surely do not belong! You overstep yourself, little man. Follow your proper path and give up the way of liberation. Look after your abandoned family and kingdom!"[2]

However, Gautama insisted that the seat in which he was sitting was only worthy of a person who had experienced spiritual labor and who was endowed with compassion. Given this, Mara challenged Gautama to provide evidence of his spiritual achievement, and he would do the same.

Gautama asked, "If you have any right to this seat then what witnesses do you have that you have practice the ten virtues?[3]

Mara demonstrated his authority when he commanded his soldiers and servants to attest to his advanced spirituality, and they answered unanimously, "I am his witness."[4]

"What witnesses do you have?" Mara lashed out.[5]

Gautama stood alone before Mara and his soldiers. Although he didn't say a single word, he used his inner power to ask for support. Gautama asked for help within his heart as he drew his right hand forward and touched the ground. To the surprise of all those present, the ground answered with a thundering cry, "I bear you witness." The sound of the thundering earth caused fear and confusion among the herd of elephants, which dropped Mara and his soldiers to the ground before running away in all directions.[6]

Gautama had not used the power of his ego. Instead, he enlisted the "forces of nature" to remove the obstacles standing in his way to enlightenment. This struggle of forces showed Gautama that he had the ability to create the change he desired, not through the power of the ego, but through the empowerment of inner truth.

When Gautama touched the ground and caused the earth to tremble, he had experienced his first epiphany. He realized that he had great power to accomplish his spiritual goal in spite of all odds. Gautama then had the confidence to believe in his mission. He knew that he would have resistance and oppositional forces, such as Mara, but now he would have the emotional strength to resist.

Gautama's meeting with Mara was similar in nature to Jesus' encounter with the devil. They were both threatened by the evil force of resistance, which raised self-doubt and fear about their missions. Both realized that they must focus their attention on spiritual fulfillment rather than satisfying their own needs. Buddha had once considered going home and quitting. Receiving the empowerment from the earth was a huge motivation for him to continue on his journey. He now knew that he was on the right path, no matter how challenging it might seem.

Gautama realized that Mara was only one of the many more who would object and doubt him. During his first years leading his own Sangha, Gautama experienced resistance from many people who didn't believe in his work. His followers advised him to move to a different city so they could function better, but Gautama who became Buddha replied, "No Ananda, there will be no end in that way. We had better remain here and bear the abuse patiently until it ceases...The Enlightened One is not controlled by these external things."[7]

Gautama had a strong faith in his passion and his mission. No obstacle would stop him from doing his mission. After the confrontation with Mara, Gautama took the time to reflect on his mission before he took the next step.

Gautama, confused and lacking direction, made his way to the village of Senayani near the Nairañjanā River. This spacious land reminded Gautama of the tranquility he had experienced one day in his childhood while seated under a rose apple tree. Gautama sat under the Bodhi tree in the asana (cross-legged) position for forty-nine days and vowed not to move from the spot until he had reached the state of nirvana.[8]

"I will not uncross my legs until the destruction of defilements has been attained."[9]

I imagine that during his meditation, he saw his life as a "movie," playing through his imagination. Then Gautama had another epiphany: "Of course, how could I have been so blind!" he exclaimed.[10]

Gautama found The Middle Way, comparing his old life as a prince and his new life as a hermit. Both experiences held the key for his awakening.

The extreme life of pleasure does not motivate a person to look for life meaning and improve reality.

Why fix something that is not broken? he asked.

The extreme austerity lifestyle only leads to frustration when one goes beyond normal effort to connect to his higher self while neglecting his existing self.

If the extreme directions did not work, there must be a middle way between the austerity and indulgence, Gautama concluded.

Both these extreme lifestyles led Gautama to think about an easy way to achieve liberation. He soon arrived at the conclusion that a little bit of effort to be mindful was all that was needed before the middle way would become second nature.

In this moment, Gautama understood that the truth he was searching for comes from within, but he hadn't been able to see it until he viewed his experiences and all that he had learned. He concluded that the truth was not absolute nor an objective fact that fits all humans. Instead, it was a personal truth unique to each person's experiences and life lessons. For

Gautama, that truth flowed from the extremes of his two lifestyles. Now he knew that people could, in fact, change the condition of suffering if they listen to their inner truth that is revealed through their life experiences.

His best advice to his students was to listen to their own voices. Their inner truth would support their progress and guide them to fulfillment. Gautama spoke with his most loyal assistant, leaving him his legacy:

"I am now old, Ananda, 80 years old. As a worn-out cart has to be kept going by repairs, so it seems to me, the body of the Tathagata can only be kept going by repairs. Therefore, Ananda, dwell making yourselves your island (support), making yourselves, not anyone else, your refuge; making the dharma your island (support), the dharma your refuge, nothing else your refuge."[11]

Step 5: Epiphany

Moses:
Choosing to Be a Hebrew

Moses settled down in Midian to lead the life of a shepherd. He sat in the desert by himself, day in and day out, giving himself an opportunity to be alone and think about his life. Although he was proud of the life he had established in Midian and grateful for the peace he found there, he couldn't help but wonder about the pain of the suffering Hebrews who were still under the repressive yoke of the pharaoh in Egypt.

One day in the desert, Moses noticed an illogical mirage. "An angel of the Lord appeared to him in a blazing fire out of a bush. He gazed, and there was a bush all aflame, yet the bush was not consumed."[12]

The desert plant, which remained whole inside the flame, attracted his attention. He knew it held some special meaning for him. Moses said, "I must turn aside to look at this marvelous sight..."[13]

Moses' interest in the burning bush symbolized his intention to get closer to his true self. It is reasonable to assume that this event was just one in a chain of revelation events that compelled Moses to become more closely acquainted with his truth.

I believe that every time Moses went to the desert, he quieted his mind and meditated. Each time, he had a different vision—a different form of communication with his higher self.

According to the Scriptures of the Torah, the sight of the burning bush drew Moses' attention to a direct encounter with God's angel. "An angel of the Lord appeared to him in blazing fire out of a bush."[14] This external appearance of the burning bush symbolized an internal burning for introspection. It was an internal voice calling for Moses to look within. "Moses, Moses."[15] Moses immediately answered, "Here I am,"[16] which established his intention to look within his true self.

I am looking at myself and my life to learn if this is what I need to do for the rest of my life, he asked himself.

Moses then studied his memories. He had not, in his heart of hearts, desired to leave his old way of life in Egypt, but the discrimination had forced his hand and undermined his natural sense of belonging. His life in Midian was certainly more peaceful since he became a respected member of an esteemed tribe, which had endowed him with some measure of peace and tranquility. However, something still nagged at him. Apparently, living an everyday, pedestrian life in Midian did not satisfy Moses' deeper hunger to contribute to the world at large in a greater spiritual way. Up until then, Moses had fulfilled his existing self, but he didn't have a chance to satisfy and express his spiritual essence as a leader of justice.

I assume that Moses asked himself the question:

When was the last time I felt a sense of satisfaction from something I did? *he asked*

Moses' first epiphany happened when he remembered the great moment of satisfaction as he defended the slave from the abusive Egyptian. This "light bulb moment" was similar to the vision Buddha had as he remembered the compassionate moment in his childhood. Both men had experienced an unselfish moment in their past, which didn't result in any personal gain. But the strong sense of satisfaction they had felt as a result was the most significant moment in their lives. This made them realize that happiness doesn't come from what we accumulate and receive, but from compassion and the act of giving.

This memory assisted Moses to identify his truth and discover his calling, so I believe he thought:

That is what I want to do for the rest of my life. That is what is lacking from my "perfect" life in Midian, he thought.

As he continued to think about it, Moses had experienced another epiphany.

I believe that Moses came to the conclusion on his own that he had to continue his mission of promoting social justice. He understood that his past attempts to change the policy of social inequality in Egypt were doomed because the Egyptian people, who enjoyed the advantage of power, did not desire this change. Moses reasoned that a way to loosen the oppressive regime was to join the ranks of the oppressed and inspire them with the hopes of redemption.

Through his internal dialogue, Moses considered the possibility of returning to Egypt, not as a former member of the Egyptian elite, but as a slave fighting for the rights of his brothers. If he would go back to Egypt as a Hebrew who desired to change its destiny, he would have a good chance to achieve this goal.

In spite of the written version that God had revealed His plan and sent Moses on a mission, I tend to believe that Moses considered changing his identity willingly to achieve their common goals of liberation and justice. Only among the Hebrews could he fulfill his calling and live his truth. At this stage, Moses voluntarily severed his link of destiny to the Egyptian people and the royal family he had been born into, and replaced it with an empathic link to the slaves.

It is my own opinion that circumstances about Moses' birth as a Hebrew were created to justify Moses' destiny as a future leader of the Hebrews that he was originally one of their own. But, I personally prefer to think that Moses chose his destiny through his revelation, and he was one hundred percent committed to establishing his passion, and not because God had assigned him.

Moses chose to be a Hebrew so he could make a difference. Still, he was unclear about his plan of action and certainly had fears about how he would achieve his goal. His inner dialogue continued to communicate his worries and fears.

In Midian, Moses had observed his father-in-law meting out justice to the members of the tribe. From this experience, he concluded that social discrimination could be avoided by the implementation of law. This idea gave Moses the inspiration to liberate the slaves in order to create an ideal society—one in which all people are obligated to obey common law, which serves the common ground.

At this point, Moses realized that Midian was a temporary place where he became aware of his passion and learned skills of leadership, but it was not a place where he could see himself living forever. The life in Midian was like a tunnel that led him forward, but not to his destination. He could not remain there if he couldn't fulfill his passion for leadership.

This growing realization was what led him to choose to become a Hebrew and carry on a new identity that he would have the rest of his life.

The Hebrew community is the perfect place where I could serve, educate, and guide in order to fulfill my passion as a leader, Moses thought.

In his mind, he envisioned the entire journey—starting from the fight of liberation and ending with the establishment of a new nation. Moses truly wished to establish his own community and take them on a journey of liberation through the establishment of a new nation based on law and justice.

Step 5: Epiphany

Jesus:
Living by the Essence of Love

Jesus' inclination to stay at the temple and study the wisdom of the Scriptures as a child[17]—and later on as an adult—only increased when he heard about John the Baptist, the prophet from the Jordan Valley who advocated repentance and baptized sinners in the Jordan River to purify their souls.

John's demand for moral penitence made an impression on the young Jesus, who understood that spiritual redemption does not depend on God's acts of miracles but on human effort once an individual has come to understand that he or she must mend his or her ways. Human harmony, which John the Baptist called "God's Kingdom," was therefore attainable.

Jesus' first epiphany was stimulated by his encounter with John the Baptist in the year 26 BCE. Immediately after Jesus' baptism, the gates of heaven opened and the spirit of God hovered before him like a dove in the sky. "After baptism Jesus came up out of the water at once, and at that moment heaven opened; he saw the Spirit of God descending like a dove to alight upon him…"[18]

Afterward, Jesus felt the need to be alone in order to reflect more deeply on the message of John the Baptist. "Repent; for the kingdom of Heaven is upon you!"[19]

What is the exact nature of the Kingdom? What is required to attain it? How can human beings implement the Kingdom of God? How will human beings redeem themselves from society's weaknesses? Jesus wondered.

Jesus was guided by the Holy Spirit to go to the desert where he underwent a spiritual test.

The Scriptures are missing the entire year between the fall of 26 and the fall of 27 BCE, which indicates a longer stay in the desert for the purpose of thinking about his life direction.[20] As we can see from the Masters' journeys, living by our truth requires a radical change in our lives, during which one has to consider carefully all the risks and challenges.

Jesus stayed in the desert for forty days, during which time he was tempted by the devil, which symbolized an internal struggle between his physical and spiritual self. Jesus had to quiet himself in order to reflect on the most common question we all ask ourselves at least once in our lifetime.

Am I here to fulfill my own needs of survival, or am I here to fulfill my passion for a higher calling? What is really more important? he asked himself.

The devil attempted to divert Jesus from his spiritual reflections and wished to challenge him. "If you are the son of God, tell this stone to become bread."[21]

This command metaphorically represented the choice before Jesus: continue to live the life of the flesh and ignore his spiritual calling, or fulfill his spiritual calling, thereby benefiting all of humanity. Which one would prevail? Jesus rejected the devil's offer, saying, "Man cannot live on bread alone."[22]

Jesus then sank into meditation, focusing on the spiritual mandate that had been presented to him.

What can I do to make the world a better place? he asked.

He recognized his natural abilities as a teacher and healer, through which he could fulfill the mandate he was contemplating.

I should not focus my effort to satisfy my body; helping people and using my gift is satisfying my soul, he thought.

However, the devil had not given up on his attempts to divert Jesus' attention from his meditation. He promised Jesus social popularity, economic bounty, and an honorable position in his community, all of which were designed to appeal to the ego.

In a flash, the devil showed Jesus all the kingdoms of the world. "All this dominion will I give to you," he said, "and the glory that goes with it... You have only to do homage to me and it shall be yours."[23]

This time, the devil tried to convince Jesus to surrender to the temptation of matter, which would divert him from his spiritual work and enslave him in a perpetual chase for material goods and achievements. This inner conflict indicates the very real human struggle between the need to feed the ego and the wish to give our lives in service to the larger community. Jesus, like any normal human being, desired public popularity, an honorable position, and even material abundance. But his passion for addressing moral weaknesses compelled him to suppress his personal interests in favor of helping humanity.

I must love my fellow man more than I love myself, he thought.

The realization that one must love others more than oneself was Jesus' epiphany. Jesus became aware that serving and leaving a legacy leaves a mark on this world, whereas serving ourselves is forgettable and meaningless. The only way one could fulfill oneself in this lifetime is if one fulfills his spiritual essence.

Jesus continued to communicate this message by claiming, "No servant can be the slave of two masters; for either he will hate the first and love the second, or he will be devoted to the first and think nothing of the second. You cannot serve God and Money."[24]

According to Jesus' experience, if you are living your life to satisfy your own needs, you worship yourself—"your inner devil." But if you acknowledge that you have a gift and the ability to help others and improve the world, then you are fully devoted to God and are actively fulfilling your spiritual vocation. That is the true meaning of his words, "You shall do homage to the Lord your God and worship Him alone."[25]

Jesus wished to impart a new morality to humanity—one not founded on laws and customs, but on the supreme value of love. Jesus hoped to be courageous enough to continue on his spiritual path, but he doubted himself and was afraid of the resistance his new decisions might bring. Jesus, like Muhammad, knew that breaking away from tradition was a big step and one that he needed to be completely ready to undertake.

The devil recognized Jesus' weakness and took this opportunity to undermine his confidence. "If you are the son of God," he said, "throw yourself down; for Scripture says, 'He will give his angels order to take care of you,' and again, 'They will support you in their arms for fear you should strike your foot against a stone.'"[26]

This was the hardest challenge that caused Jesus to struggle against his own fate.

Should I accept my fate as a Jew to adhere to the tradition of my ancestors, or should I follow my truth, which urges me to change my way of life? he asked.

Jesus realized that he had a radical vision for humanity, but if he would fulfill his yearning for social reform, he would have to be ready for social struggle—and if he did not realize his yearning, his internal struggle would continue. Either way, he was in conflict, which obligated him to make a decision. Jesus chose to trust his spiritual calling, which led him to announce, "You are not to put the Lord your God to the test."[27]

Having faith in his spiritual calling empowered Jesus with divine force to accomplish his goal, regardless of the challenges that were due to come his way.

After that, Jesus devoted his life to publicizing his message inspired by John. "Repent; for the kingdom of heaven is upon you!"[28]

Jesus' call for repentance underscored his yearning for essential reform of the society in which he lived.[29] Jesus did not ask the faithful to confess their sins, but to perform an essential change in their social conduct. He demanded that people suppress their intention to sin before committing the act in question itself; he bequeathed to them the concept of the "extra mile," which was designed to extend the effort of giving beyond what was required by Jewish law; and he demanded they offer love instead of resistance in the face of an enemy's hostility. Jesus also asked that people mete out leniency in the face of transgressions.

Jesus hoped that the ensuing changes in social behavior would not only secure the Kingdom of God for the individual enacting those changes, but it would also create a society that functioned in an ideal way.

Step 5: Epiphany

Muhammad:
Submitting to Al Llah

Muhammad made long trips as a merchant. Often during his journeys, he would spend many days by himself in a cave on Mount Hira before returning home. One night, Muhammad had a dream, which left its impression on him:

"The first revelation that was granted to the messenger of Allah was the true dream in a state of sleep, so that he never dreamed a dream but the truth of it shone forth like the dawn of the morning. Then solitude became dear to him, and he used to seclude himself in the cave of Hira"[30]

Muhammad returned frequently to visit the cave, where he continued to maintain inner communication, which was designed to clarify the purpose of his life. In the year 610 CE, the angel, Gabriel, was revealed to him. "Whilst I was walking along, I heard a voice from heaven and I raised my eyes, and lo! The angel that had appeared to me in Hira was sitting on a throne between heaven and earth and I was struck with awe on account of him and returned home..."[31]

This odd vantage point between heaven and earth indicates Muhammad's meditative state of mind. During his introspective vision, Muhammad heard a voice that penetrated his internal consciousness and directed the focus of his attention.

"So the angel came to him and said, 'Read.'"[32] Muhammad, stricken with terror and fear, refused to read the message because he could not read nor write. Muhammad said, "I am not the one who can read."[33] And he continued, "Then he (the angel) took hold of me and he pressed me so hard that I could not bear it anymore, and then he let me go and said, 'Read.'"[34]

We can assume that Muhammad's illiteracy was a legitimate reason why he rejected the angel's admonitions to read the message, but the angel of God did not give up, knowing that Muhammad would eventually face his truth. He held Muhammad again, and on the third time increased the pressure even more to convince Muhammad to surrender to the message of God.

Karen Armstrong, in *Muhammad: A Biography of the Prophet,* defines the event as "spiritual rape." The sense of strain is familiar from God's revelations before the prophets of Israel, which appear in the Scriptures.

Armstrong explains that the sense of strain indicates the prophet's spiritual transcendence to a sublime spiritual dimension.[35]

I agree that this was the outcome of this revelation, but I tend to believe that the sense of strain, which Muhammad describes in his own words, derives instead from Muhammad's inner dilemma.

Do I cling to my heart's desire, which contradicts my tribe's norm? Or should I relinquish my world-view in order to live in harmony with my kinship community? he asked.

In his truth, Muhammad indeed wanted to "read aloud" the message of God—to announce his faith openly. He wanted to reveal his intention in public, which would allow him to follow God's way, but he was concerned about the practical implications of his decision.

The angel of God, symbolizing Muhammad's internal voice, repeated his request three times in order to check Muhammad's intention.

Are you certain? Do you really desire the change? the Angel asked.

The recurring, intensifying strain clarified to Muhammad that he had no choice but to act according to the decree of his conscience. "...Then he took hold of me and pressed me hard for the third time, then he let go and said, 'Read in the name of thy Lord who created...'"[36]

Muhammad opened his mouth to recite the message and declared his intention to make a radical change in his life. Muhammad said in his own words, "It was as though the words were written on my heart."[37]

Muhammad's statement supports my observation that he didn't read anything, but rather said what was in his heart and mind. "Recite in the name of thy Lord who created man from a clot and thy Lord is most honorable."[38]

This moment of truth as a result of the angel's persistence was Muhammad's epiphany. Muhammad finally admitted to himself loud and clear what he believed in. He had to honor it and live by it. There was no other way he could live his life.

Muhammad had already accomplished a change of lifestyle prior to this revelation with the angel. He was a faithful believer of Al Llah, and he was living by His policy of justice. In general, he was already acting in opposition to the tribal norm by extending his hand to help care for the weak and by conducting himself with modesty and kindness, in contrast to the greedy exploiters in his tribe. Yet taking this one step further by making his spiritual intentions public required courage. It demanded that he carry out a radical change in his way of life.

Am I the most suitable person for this vocation? Muhammad pondered.

Upon his return home, Muhammad told his wife about the revelation and his fears.

He came to Khadija trembling and said, "Wrap me up, wrap me up." She wrapped him up until the awe left him. Then he related to her what had happened. "I fear for myself."[39]

Khadija, his wife, listened to her husband. She then told him that he needed not be afraid to take the next step since his actions were the realization of his true calling. Khadija said, "Nay. By Allah, Allah will never bring thee to disgrace, for thou unitest the tie of relationship and bearest the burden of the weak and earnest for the destitute and honourest the guest and helpest in real distress."[40]

Khadija consoled Muhammad and emphasized that he was already doing the work, which to her mind was an indication that he should continue on the same path. Her comforting words convinced Muhammad that he was indeed the one who could implement God's wish.

Muhammad received revelations from the angel, Gabriel, on each of his subsequent visits to the cave on Mount Hira. Muhammad said that the revelation events were painful because during each one he experienced the same pressure he had felt from Gabriel initially. "Never once did I receive a revelation without thinking that my soul had been torn away from me."[41] Muhammad accepted his mission to establish change, but this process always involved pain. He was about to hurt the people he loved and otherwise embark on an unknown journey. His pain was understandable.

Muhammad wavered about the question of fulfillment for two years. Only in the year 612 CE did Muhammad expose his identity and faith to his kindred and undertake slow and cautious steps to fulfill his spiritual purpose.[42]

The Spiritual Lesson of Epiphany

The internal dialogue with the higher self is still a part of a stagnant time period while contemplating a life-changing decision. The Masters asked themselves this fundamental question: Shall I continue to honor tradition or shall I follow my own truth? At that point in their lives, they acknowledged that their core value was radically different than the conditioning they had been brought up with. But, exposing their truth in public and living up to it was another matter altogether. If they chose to live their truth, it would upset many people, including the people they loved. They might have lost their income, popularity, and respect in the process. This fear appears in our lives as well when we are about to make a life-changing decision to live up to our truth.

Several months after I had quit my job as a teacher in the Jewish school in 2005, I took a long break to rethink my life and tried to figure out why I couldn't be a good Jew. I asked myself similar questions:

Shall I continue to accept the Jewish values that I can't accept? Or should I follow my heart's desire to emerge into the multicultural world?

My Jewish life contradicted my truth to live by the essence of oneness, and I had to decide what kind of values I would rather live by. Making this difficult decision made me feel the same sense of pressure that Muhammad had felt when he was touched by the angel, Gabriel, as a conscious pressure from within.

Was I ready to make a life changing decision?

I knew where my heart wanted to go, but changing direction meant breaking away from my Jewish family, whom I loved dearly. It meant undercutting my source of income and possibly changing a career that I had worked so hard to establish.

Was I ready to give all of that up?

The reality was that I had never lived up to my Jewish values. I had already failed to abide by the traditional expectation to structure my life around a husband and a permanent job. I had already crossed the social boundaries between Jews and gentiles, and I already had a distant relationship with my family. My true self was already winning this debate, but now I can make a conscious decision to accept my truth.

The fear of losing everything in order to make a radical change in our lives holds us back from living our truth. But in reality, the loss of an old and unhappy chapter in our lives is a beginning of a new and improved chapter. We should not focus on what we lose but on our gain. When we are no longer obligated to live by the old values, we gain freedom. At this point we are able to release ourselves from resistance and go against our own true nature, which normally shows up in our lives through conflicts with others, and all kind of challenges that are meant to test our intention to change. When we honor our truth, we will create peace and harmony in our lives. And even the people who resisted us would be able to accept the change, and they eventually would be inspired by our courage.

Last year I had witnessed it myself, when my own parents came to visit me form Israel. I brought them to my home where I live a non-Jewish life with non-Jewish housemates during the holidays. The house was full of Christmas decorations, and I didn't have a mezuzah on the door post. Yet, my parents seemed to love my housemates, they enjoyed the Christmas decorations, and they loved my choice of friends.

During this visit my mom was admitted to the hospital, and I called a friend for help. She arrived immediately. My father was so impressed and first he asked me:

"Is she Jewish?"

"No" I answered, not sure what he was going to say.

Then he said with all seriousness: "She has potential."

This powerful moment showed me that my father was able to accept my choices and, more importantly, he opened his heart and experienced my values. If I had such an impact on my father, there is hope for the rest of us.

When we live by our truth, we become aware of our higher purpose, and the impact we have around us. We are here to change and inspire change. By doing so, we are activating our Godlike potential to create and improve the world. In the end, we don't take any of our material accomplishments with us, but if we were lucky to live by our truth, we would leave our spiritual imprint on this earth. In that sense, our lives are dedicated to establishing a new direction based on the foundation of our newfound truth.

Buddha emphasized that the goal of being completely free from the illusion of self can be attained when one is truly living to serve:

"His service to others is of the purest, for he has no thought of self. He gains nothing, accumulates nothing, not even anything spiritual, because he is free from the illusion of self and the "thirst" for becoming."[38]

It is our goal and privilege to reach the powerful state of Nothingness.

A starter to implement the teaching of inner dialogue:

- Quiet your mind to eliminate the surrounding noise so you can hear your own voice.
- Ask yourself, what is holding you back from living your truth?
- Think about all the risks and the price you pay for making a radical change.
- Release the fear of loss and focus on the freedom you will gain.

PART III

CREATING A NEW AND IMPROVED LIFE

Create the highest, grandest vision possible for your life,
because you become what you believe.
~Oprah Winfrey

CHAPTER 6

AWAKENING: SPIRITUAL RE-BIRTH

You are never given a dream without also
being given the power to make it true.
~ Richard Bach

We are finally ready to shift direction, getting out of the darkness and into the light. The shift of consciousness is already happening through a transformation of values and beliefs. As a result, our core value becomes our natural state of being. We no longer just believe in it, we are it.

As we are awakened to the truth, we recognize the imperfection in reality that only we could see and acknowledge. But seeing the weakness is not enough, we have to do something about it; we have to fight for what we believe in; we must thrive to create the change that is required so we can live in peace with ourselves.

If we chose to ignore it and live our "normal" day to day lives, we are in a "sleeping mode"—going to work, doing chores, taking care of a loved one, watching TV, going to bed, and starting it all over again. The purpose of this kind of life is simply to survive. But, life is much more than that —it is about living our truth and fulfilling a higher purpose.

And so, the ending of an old chapter in our lives of focusing on surviving marks the beginning of a new chapter in our lives where we are committed to living our truth. This concept is symbolized by the biblical view of resurrection: our physical body dies and our "spiritual body" is reborn. The resurrection (awakening from death) is a metaphor of spiritual awakening that transforms lives in the here and now as we become fully aware of our truth. We can still have a normal life, but at the same time, we raise our standards and make an effort to live by our truth. This awakening state of conscious is lifting us to the level of creators, as we recognize our ability to contribute and make a difference.

Once we come to peace with our truth, we begin to activate it, making conscious choices to align our lives with it. We will invite like-minded people to join us; we will change our lifestyle to establish the conditions it needs; we will choose the right surroundings that support us. We will constantly make choices, take actions, and create the ideal life base on the newfound truth. But, we are not the only ones that are impacted by it; everyone around us is influenced by it as well.

It is not necessarily an easy journey, but the Universe will enhance and empower us to accomplish our goals beyond what we can imagine. It is much like Oprah's ability to reach out and help so many people in the world. If we would only use five percent of our spiritual truth, we would bring so much light into the world that would change the face of the Universe.

In this chapter, I will show how the Masters turned their inner truth into a life mission. As they activated their truth, they accessed their divine quality to create the world in their own spiritual image.

The transformation into higher beings is our greatest potential, and we are all capable of reaching it. The Old Testament said that we are created in the image of God—meaning that we inherited a godlike gift to create and continue the process of creation. We have the power and the responsibility to change civilizations and improve the quality of life.

Step 6: Awakening

Buddha:
Buddha is the Dharma

G autama's "near-death" experience was a turning point as he decided to put an end to his old life as a wandering hermit. His awakening was inspired by the epiphany he experienced, being detached from human influence and totally alone in a remote place where he connected to his higher self. At this point, Gautama understood that his old self no longer existed since the egoistic goals that motivated him in the past were no longer part of his life in the present.

By leaving his old life behind, Gautama had given birth to his true self.

Gautama arrived at the conclusion that he had to release himself from all the conditioning he inherited—from the social expectations and from his old identity, *Prakrti*.

Liberation from the "collective self" (inherited identity) would help him to connect to his spiritual essence, *Puresa*, which is the absolute spirit. To explain this, I must borrow a metaphor from Hindu wisdom. The absolute spirit is the "body," our authentic self, which exists in each lifetime. In every cycle of living, we wear a different "outfit," which is our current identity, influenced by inherited factors. Gautama wished to remove the "outfit," to get rid of the obstacles in his birth surroundings in order to take a better look at his authentic self.

Liberation from the past gives one permission to choose his path and to follow his heart's desire. Buddha called it "a place of bliss" when a person is completely liberated from egoistic desire. At this point, one's true happiness does not come from satisfaction of the "ego-self," but from his service to people.

"He who has realized the truth, Nirvana, is the happiest being in the world. He is free from all complexes and obsessions, the worries and troubles that torment others. His mental health is perfect. He does not repent the past, nor does he brood over the future. He lives fully in the present. Therefore he appreciates and enjoys things in the purest sense without self-projections. He is joyful, exultant, enjoying the pure life, his faculties pleased, free from anxiety, serene and peaceful. As he is free from selfish desire, hatred, ignorance, conceit, pride and all such defilements, he is pure and gentle, full of universal love, compassion, kindness, sympathy, understanding and tolerance. His service to others is of the purest, for he has no thought of self. He gains nothing, accumulates nothing, not even anything spiritual, because he is free from the illusion of self and the "thirst" for becoming."[1]

The process of rebirth, as we witness from Gautama's life, includes two parts. The first part is the death of an old self, which is the end of the first chapter where he was a normal being living a commonplace life. This path is no longer relevant. His new life will be completely different from the life he had before because his conscious state of mind had shifted. Gautama didn't see himself as a "private" person motivated by egoistic goals to satisfy his own and his family needs. He was a new person who wished to contribute to the greater good of all.

The second part is the "life after death," which is the life of an awakened being who is no longer a "private" person. He sees his mission as a messenger who is able to create the change he desires.

When Gautama quieted his mind, he surveyed and reviewed the experiences of his life. He focused on a childhood memory of an event that had taken place during an "uprooting" ceremony, designed to prepare the fields for the next planting season. He observed the ceremony and noticed the branch of an uprooted tree where an insect's eggs had been nested and now were lost. The insect's loss evoked feelings of compassion and empathy within Gautama.

"I call to mind how when my father was ploughing, I sat in the cool shade of the Rose-Apple tree remote from sensual desires and ill conditions and entered upon an abode in the First Musing, that is accompanied by thought distracted and sustained which is born of solitude, full of zestful ease."[2]

"Late at night, Gautama made a discovery:
Not nakedness, nor matted hair, nor filth
Nor fasting long, nor lying on the ground,
Not dust and dirt, nor squatting on the heels
Can cleanse the mortal that is full of doubt

But one that lives a calm and tranquil life,
Though gaily decked, if tamed, restrained he live
Walking the holy path in righteousness,
Laying aside all harm to living things,
True mendicant, ascetic, Brahmin he."[3]

Gautama finally understood that the path to enlightenment did not involve the strenuous effort he had undertaken in the past, but rather was a result of spontaneous action stemming from natural conditions as he had experienced when he was a child.[4]

Gautama reconstructed in his memory the conditions of the trance he had entered into when he was a boy. He pondered what it might mean to put his ego aside for good and give up all selfish desires.

Both his childhood memories and the contrast between two extreme lifestyles led Gautama to a breakthrough. Gautama accepted the idea of a middle path, coupled with one should be morally responsible for all of one's actions. In this manner, he was paving the way for a person to exercise self-discipline, which ideally would become second nature after a short time.[5]

Gautama inspired to change the tone of prohibitions to emphasize how easily it can be achieved through mindfulness about the things we should avoid:

1. People should avoid intended damage of any kind to their fellow man, such as murder, hate, and anger in order to strengthen the intensity of love and graciousness;

2. People should avoid taking another's property without permission in order to nurture generosity and emphasize the importance of giving;

3. People should avoid inappropriate sexual conduct in order to establish relationships based on love and harmony;

4. People should avoid lying in order to build a life of trust and truth;

5. People should avoid poisoning the body and the soul (by means of drugs or alcohol) in order to nurture internal clarity.[6]

The eternal tranquility that Gautama craved emanated from a code of conduct based on the precept of unselfish love, where a person learns to live without the restrictions of an ego. The most supreme level of a human being exists when a person is capable of showing empathy for the suffering of his fellow man and when a person is able to generate contentment from another person's pleasure.

From this point on, Gautama dedicated his life to service. Gautama fulfilled his spiritual destiny when he paved the way for liberation through the teaching of the *The Eightfold Path*, which summarized the turning points in his journey.

From being the student of suffering, Gautama turned into a teacher of liberation, which privileged him the title "Buddha, The Enlightened One."

Gautama earned his divine power that would give him the recognition he needed to spread his message. "I am a supreme king, I am the holy one beyond compare, I rejoice free from fear."[7]

Once Gautama was aware of his inner power to transcend humanity and help many people, nothing could stop him, not even fear or doubt. He did not speak from his ego but from his heart. When one is so driven and motivated to follow his truth, he does not see obstacles or fear but rather the importance of his mission.

According to Gautama's words, every person is capable of becoming "Buddha." "He who sees me sees the Dhamma, and he who sees the Dhamma sees me."[8]

The *Dhamma*, or normally *Dharma*, is one's true self; the "Buddha" is the potential of awakening.

On his deathbed he told his students, "Dear friends, my physical body will not be here tomorrow, but my teaching body (*Dharmakaya*) will always be with you."[9]

Buddha didn't intend to insulate his students from his absence after his death, but he wished to leave them with inspiration to seek their truth. His life was evidence that a man's spiritual work would leave its mark on the world even when his physical entity no longer existed. Gautama's spirit would survive forever through his teachings and his service.

Anyone who knows his or her truth has the potential to leave imprint on the world. With Gautama's inspiration, we must search for our spiritual truth so we are able to shine our light on this world.

Step 6: Awakening

Moses:
Moses is the Hebrews' Leader

I tend to believe that the communication with God behind the burning bush was not only one incident as the Scriptures said, but a chain of occurring events that happened over time. These incidents gradually gave Moses the confidence to follow his truth. The first part of the revelation was about the discovery of his truth and his calling through the inner communication, as mentioned in the previous chapter. The second part of this inner communication was about the fears and worries that this journey would involve.

Before Moses could take action of any kind, he first had to learn about his chosen identity as a Hebrew since he needed to gain the Hebrews' trust and respect in order to succeed in his mission. According to the Torah, God exposed the truth about Moses' identity and pointed out his biological connection to the slaves. "'I am,' He said, 'the God of your father, the God of Abraham, the God of Isaac and the God of Jacob.'"[10]

God's affinity with Abraham, Isaac, and Jacob gave Moses the cultural information and the history link that Moses needed to understand before speaking to his people. Moses needed to find a way to learn about Abraham, Isaac, and Jacob, and how to gain the trust of his people through the knowledge about their history.

Moses covered his face in dread. "And Moses hid his face, for he was afraid to look at God."[11]

Moses' reaction of hiding his face was based on a commonly held belief that "Man shall not see Me and live."[12]

I tend to believe that Moses' fear of death is symbolic since the impact of his inner communication resulted with the end of his life in Midian. It is not an actual death but rather the end of his old identity as a Midiani man.

This was the second time in Moses' life that he was changing his life's direction. He was afraid to lose his family, his connections, and the peace that he achieved in Midian, but he recognized that his life in Midian lacked purpose, and he could no longer be happy as a simple family man. He could still use his skills of being a good family man elsewhere, following his true calling to become a leader.

Under different circumstances, Muhammad had a similar moment of revelation, standing face-to-face with God, unable to recognize himself.[13] He could not believe that he was the same person that he had been in the past. He was no longer the simple man with a simple life goal, but the driven leader who wished to fight for what he believed in.

The amazing similarities between the two figures indicated a turning point in their lives when they began to believe in their divine ability to make a difference. Muhammad moved right after the incident to a new city where he started his mission, and Moses was on his way back to Egypt to liberate the Hebrew slaves.

By this time, Moses had already started the planning of his mission, but the inner communication continued to address more issues of how to execute his plan. Moses still had fears and doubts, which he expressed: "Moses said to God, 'When I come to the Israelites and say to them, 'The God of your father has sent me to you,' and they ask me, 'What is His name?' what shall I say to them?'"[14]

This question clearly indicated that Moses was taking the first step of accepting his new identity, but he was afraid to reveal his "new self"—that of a social reformer and visionary leader. Moses chose to be a Hebrew, but he still had no idea how to be one—he had to be able to clearly see himself as a Hebrew.

Moses needed an inside person who would fill this role. The Bible didn't tell us anything about how and when Moses met Aaron, who was considered to be his biological brother.[15] Aaron and Moses met as relatives, and the text only said that they have been exchanging messages from God. I tend to believe that Moses searched for an ally to educate him about the Hebrews and help him to gain their trust. He "accidentally" met Aaron when he traveled back to Egypt and formulated a strong friendship with him. The Universe was attentive to Moses' wish since he was truly passionate about his ability to change and lead.

I tend to believe that this relationship was not a biological one, but rather Moses' tactical decision that would enable him to succeed in his mission. Aaron was an inside source who helped educate Moses about the life of Hebrews. He probably taught him the figures of speech and helped him understand the cultural mindset and history. When Moses established this strong connection and gained confidence about his mission, he was ready to begin his journey as a leader.

Now that Moses had "given birth" to his new identity, he could see himself as a Hebrew. By embracing his new self as a Hebrew, Moses elevated himself to a new level as a leader, dedicated to a public mission. Moses had never neglected his obligation to his family, but now he carried much bigger responsibility as a leader and a public figure.

After the inner dialogue in the desert, Moses returned home and announced to his family that he was leaving Midian to fulfill the social vocation he was destined to carry out in Egypt. "Moses went back to his father-in-law, Jethro, and said to him, 'Let me go back to my kinsmen in Egypt and see how they are faring.'"[16]

Moses' passion and devotion to the mission of justice empowered him to overcome obstacles as he fought the resisting pharaoh and his skilled army with persistence, and led the people of Israel on a tough journey through the desert. Moses, like Jesus, performed miracles with the help of a higher power to remove obstacles and deal with challenges, such as the opening of the Red Sea,[17] striking the rock for water,[18] and distracting the Egyptian's attention with the ten plagues before escaping Egypt.

The ability to perform miracles comes from the power of manifesting, which empowers every person who follows his or her passion. Everything is possible when one believes in his or her mission and does everything to make it happen.

Step 6: Awakening

Jesus:
Jesus Reborn as the Son of God

J esus was a simple man who came from a very poor family. He was the son of Mary and Joseph, but he was not Joseph's biological son since Mary was pregnant prior to her engagement to Joseph. Without getting into the argument of who the biological father of Jesus was, Joseph accepted Jesus as his son and raised him.

Joseph was much older than his wife Mary. He was not mentioned in the Scriptures as Jesus matured into adulthood. It was most likely that Joseph died when Jesus was a teenager.[18] Mary had more children, four boys and two girls, which she probably had from a new husband—most likely Joseph's brother who had fulfilled the Torah law of Levirate marriage, according to which the unmarried brother of the deceased was obligated to marry the widow so the dead brother's name and lineage would not perish.[19] Tabor, author of *The Jesus Dynasty,* suggested that Mary was remarried to Joseph's brother, Clophas.[20] Clophas' name was indeed mentioned in the Scriptures.[21]

Jesus, as the firstborn son, took the responsibility of providing for his family. Even though we have no idea what Jesus did for a living before his mission at the age of thirty, we can assume that he learned the skills of a builder from his father. We were told that Joseph was a carpenter, which actually means "builder."[22]

It is reasonable to assume that Joseph and Jesus were engaged in building the town of Sepphoris[23] since Harod Atipas used laborers to build a modern town in the Galilee, and Jesus continued to do so after his father's death. This assumption is supported by the fact that Jesus was very familiar with the adversity of the poor, speaking from his own experiences.[24]

Jesus lived like an ordinary human being who struggled to make a living, faced family crises, and so on. The adversities of poverty he experienced helped him see the need for a compassionate approach toward the sinners who were compelled to commit a sin because of their lack of means. He wished to help the weak and the poor to live with dignity. Jesus hoped for a better way to improve life—his and others.

Jesus' wish came to fruition when he met John the Baptist and listened to his message. John's words resonated with Jesus who was seeking change.

When Jesus returned from the wilderness, he was a different person. He was no longer an average man who strived to achieve trivial life goals. He rose beyond it, demonstrating the importance of giving and serving people with his spiritual gift. From this point on, Jesus believed in his mission to serve people through healing and teaching.

Jesus' healings included curing the paralytic and the deaf, restoring sight to the blind, and removing negative energy (demons). He spent a great deal of his time teaching through parables and preaching in the synagogue. Jesus finally found his passion and developed his craft through his mission. He shared his spiritual teachings with his disciples and trained them to be healers and teachers so they would continue to carry on the legacy of his work.

Jesus' dedication to public service turned him into an omnipotent figure with the ability to change life simply by living his truth. The miracles that Jesus performed as a healer established his renown as the Son of God, graced with supreme accreditation from a higher power, which only enhanced his natural ability as a gifted healer. This higher force of support grew even bigger as Jesus continued to develop his craft and heal more people. Jesus was in fact a divine human being in that sense. But in truth, every person, who is using his talent to improve life, has a divine empowerment to enforce it.

Through Jesus' inspiration, we learn that every person who focuses his or her goals on giving has the potential to be godlike. Jesus once discussed this matter with a member of the Jewish council, Nicodemus. Jesus explained to him that a man is born twice during his lifetime: once as a baby, and the second time, not in physical form but in a spiritual sense. The rebirth indicates the beginning of a new chapter, when one is fully aware of his spiritual purpose and from that point on, is shifting his attention to fulfilling his calling.

"Rabbi," he said, "we know that you are the teacher sent by God..." Jesus answered..."I tell you, unless a man has been born over again he cannot see the kingdom of God." "But how is it possible," said Nicodemus, "for a man to be born when he is old? Can he enter his mother's womb a second time and be born?" Jesus answered..."No one can enter the kingdom of God without being born from water and spirit. Flesh can give birth only to flesh; it is spirit that gives birth to spirit."[25]

Spiritual rebirth is a normal phase of every human being who shifts his or her attention from achieving egoistic goals, that only satisfy his or her own needs, to fulfilling his or her spiritual calling. This shift indicates an awakening from a state of "average" into a higher realm of consciousness, which gives one the ability to be the creator of a new vision.

Jesus encouraged his followers to look within themselves to find their inner truth, through which they would contribute to make the world a better place. "...seek, and you will find..."[26] This, he told them, was the ultimate purpose of creation.

Jesus didn't clarify what it was that the seekers were looking for, or what it was that they would find. But he promised the doors would open up in front of those who seek direction. "...He who seek finds, and to him who knocks, the door will be opened."[27]

Jesus couldn't define the destination of the journey since the destination was formulated by the individual's inclination. Yet he assured the seekers that the information they were seeking comes from within, just as Gautama had claimed. The hidden information would be discovered throughout our own life experiences as we acknowledge our own truth according to *The Gospel of Thomas.* "Recognize what is right in front of you, and that which is hidden from you will be revealed to you. Nothing hidden will fail to be displayed."[28]

Just as Jesus promised, a man who followed his truth was most likely to find his destination. Jesus reached this conclusion based on his own experiences, as he recognized his own desire to realize the principle of love and compassion declared on social reform. Jesus warned his followers about the challenges of implementing their hearts' desires, just as he had to face his protesters. It is not an easy journey, as we can learn from the *Gospel of Thomas.*

Jesus summarized the journey of seeking truth. "The seeker should not stop until he finds. When he does find, he will be disturbed. After having been disturbed, he will be astonished. Then he will reign over everything."[29]

The first step to self-discovery is shocking since one is trapped between the two worlds of the values one is raised on and the values one longs for. One can't give up on old life without an emotional destruction that shocks the old foundation. This phase is extremely important and necessary to rebuild and reconstruct. Jesus described this process of his personal circumstances as one who was trapped between the traditional Jewish streams that followed the Jewish law to the letter, and his own moral standards of acting beyond the Jewish law in order to improve the quality of life.

Jesus himself was Jewish from the day he was born to the day he died, but he was certainly "born again" during his lifetime, following his heart's desire to establish a new direction. Jesus chose to liberate himself from the obligation to follow the norm. He broke all the laws that contradicted the principle of compassion. Jesus conducted a way of life based on his own truth in spite of the resistance of his protesters.

When Jesus started his mission, his actions and principles irritated the leaders of the congregation and made him a target of hatred. For them, breaking the Jewish law and spreading a prophecy about destruction were blasphemy. They concluded that Jesus should be judged by the Jewish authority, so he was brought into the house of the highest priest who investigated and heard the accusations brought against him.

Jesus listened to his accusers who said, "You would pull the temple down, would you, and build it in three days? Come down from the cross and save yourself, if you are indeed the Son of God." So, too, the chief priest with the lawyers and the elders mocked him. "He saved others," they said, "but he cannot save himself."[30]

Jesus, however, never wished to save his own soul. Instead, he wanted to save society from self-destruction. For him, sacrifice was the noblest act of love. "Greater love has no man than this, that a man lay down his life for his friends."[31]

Jesus left a spiritual legacy, which continues to evolve and be enforced all these years after his death.

Every person who changes his or her destiny by following his or her inner truth has the ability to create the world in his or her spiritual image. Jesus said it in his own words: "When you see someone not born from a woman, prostrate yourself and worship him; he is your father."[32]

Jesus was referring to the spiritual rebirth of a person who created a new form of life after activating his or her truth and dedicated his or her life for an essential purpose. Creating the world in our own image was our divine ability.

Step 6: Awakening

Muhammad:
Muhammad is a Prophet of God

Muhammad lost his best friend and biggest supporter, his wife, Khadija, in 619 CE. Not long after her death, his beloved uncle, Abu Talib, faced death too. Muhammad was sad and felt hopeless in the face of losing the protection provided by his uncle—he could not continue living in Mecca without such protection. Muhammad's time of personal crisis was compounded by the humiliation he experienced from the community. He was frustrated that all his attempts to find allies in the city of Ta'if failed as the crowd chased him down to insult him.[33]

It was as though his old life was over, but he couldn't see how to continue and was confused about his future.

Muhammad found refuge in a private orchard, begging Al Llah for help:

"O God, unto thee do I complain of my weakness, of my helplessness and of my lowliness before man. O most Merciful of the merciful, thou art my Lord. Into whose hands wilt thou entrust me? Unto some far-off stranger who will ill treat me?...I take refuge in the light of thy Countenance whereby all darknesses are illuminated and the things of this world and the next are rightly ordered...There is no power and no might except through Thee."[34]

Muhammad was on his way back to Mecca, but he could not enter the city without protection. He wrote a petition to Mutim, the chief of Newfal, who the next day came armed to escort Muhammad to Mecca.[35]

While staying in Mecca, Muhammad visited his cousin, Umm Hani, who lived close to the Ka'aba. In the middle of the night, Muhammad rose and went to the Ka'aba to recite the Quran. Muhammad fell asleep in the back of the mosque. Suddenly he woke up with a gentle touch from the angel, Gabriel:

"Whilst I was sleeping in the Hijr...Gabriel came to me and spurred me with his foot whereupon I set upright, yet I saw nothing and lay down once again. A second time he came; and a third time and then he took me by the arm and I rose and stood beside him, and he led me out to the gate of the Mosque and there was a white beast between a mule and an ass.

With wings at his sides wherewith he moved his legs; and his every stride was as far as his eyes could see."[36]

Muhammad mounted the mysterious beast, the buruq, and flew with Gabriel to Jerusalem. This event was called *al-masjid al-aqsa* in Quran, but it was also known as the Night Journey, the Miraj.

At his arrival in Jerusalem, Muhammad joined the great prophets for a prayer on the Temple Mount. Then he climbed a ladder, arriving at a sacred place known as Heaven as he began to ascend to the Throne of God.[37]

Heaven was a divided place separated by different levels of divinity. At each stage, Muhammad met one of the great prophets: first was Adam; Jesus and John the Baptist were the second; Joseph was the third; Enoch was the fourth; Aaron and Moses in the fifth and the sixth; and Abraham in the seventh and the highest divine sphere.

The Night Journey was a spiritual experience where Muhammad transcended spiritually to a higher being. It was also where he was welcomed by other prophets who also became higher beings in their lifetimes. Muhammad proved by his own actions that he was no longer an average man who focused on the trivial goals for the sake of his own satisfaction. He risked his own life, career, family, and popularity to fight for his vision. He dedicated his life to living his truth and fulfilling his calling, which benefited society in the long term. Muhammad deserved this recognition that would empower him to continue and not give up on his mission in spite of the challenges he was facing. Muhammad finally arrived at the highest level where he met directly with God. Muhammad described his fearful anticipation:

> "He heard a call, a message from the friend.
> A call from the Essence of the All:
> Leave soul and body, transitory one!
> You, O My goal and purpose enter now
> And see My essence face to face, My friend!
> In awe, he lost his speech and lost himself—
> Muhammad did not know that Muhammad here,
> Saw not himself—He saw Soul of the Souls,
> The face of Him who made the universe."[38]

Muhammad left his body and soul before he met with God as though he was dead. Karen Armstrong, author of *Muhammad: A Biography of the Prophet,* referred to the old belief that whoever saw God in person would die. Muhammad was afraid for his life in meeting God face-to-face, but he didn't die and returned to Mecca right after the Night Journey. Muhammad realized that during this transition, it was his old self that was dying, not his physical self. Armstrong supported this claim.[39] This event marked Muhammad's rebirth as a prophet and messenger of God, as his old life as an "average" being was over.

When Muhammad was standing in the presence of God, he did not recognize his old self; he had indeed reached a turning point in his life. But something else happened during the meeting with God: Muhammad saw himself not only face-to-face with God but soul-to-soul—a much deeper level of connection. He saw himself as an equal to God. Muhammad never claimed that he was the son of God, but he recognized his divine potential to become godlike. He had the ability to create the world in his own spiritual image. Muhammad expressed this realization when he said, "Whoever sees me has seen God."[40]

Muhammad knew that he was as divine and powerful as God since he received the divine inspiration to create and improve the world in his own image through his vision.

Muhammad followed his spiritual calling, learning about the essence of his true self. He realized for the first time that human beings had the same divine quality to create and improve life on earth, which empowered him to return with enthusiasm to fulfill his spiritual calling.

As soon as this event ended, Muhammad returned to Mecca, but his life started to take a different direction. He made a pact with six men from the city of Yathrib, whom he met during the Hajji in 620 CE. They agreed to accept the message of Islam and gave him their word that he would be welcomed in the small oasis of Yathrib since they already knew about the coming of the prophet from Arabia from their Jewish tribes.[41]

Muhammad left Mecca in 622 CE and moved to reestablish his life in the city of Yathrib, which changed its name to Medina, "The City." This was where the prophet established his first community of Muslims. Muhammad took more practical steps to realize his vision. At first, he brought the Muslim immigrants from Abyssinia who were forced to leave Mecca, and continued his teaching to attract a new audience. But the most significant thing he did was establishing a new community of Muslims called the *Umma*, which was the first community of people who were not blood-related. They came together to live by the new faith of Islam. The

Hajira event symbolized Muhammad's spiritual rebirth as he lived a fully awakened life dedicated to his mission.

From the Hadith of Gabriel, we learned that Muhammad was approached by an old man while traveling in the oasis of Medina. The old man kneeled as a sign of respect and recognized Muhammad by his name.[42] The old man was the angel Gabriel who came to ask Muhammad about the coming of the Judgment Day, a day that would bring the biggest change in history. Muhammad answered with a metaphor that this day will come when "The slave girl will give birth to her mistress."[43]

Muhammad used this metaphor to explain that people can change their destiny simply by living their truth as he did. The girl was born as a slave, yet she changed her destiny by giving birth to her true self, the "Master." By doing so, she released herself from her destiny as a slave and was able to create her own life.

The slave girl resembled the virgin mother who gave birth to the son of God. In both cases, a spiritual rebirth is an indication of a turning point when one is fully aware of his or her spiritual calling. From this point on, one is creating the world in his or her own spiritual image.

Taking responsibility for our own destiny is what makes us divine. It is our responsibility to ask ourselves what is wrong in our own backyard and how we can resolve it.

The Spiritual Lesson of Awakening

The awakening phase in our lives begins when we become committed to live our truth. Every day upon waking up in the morning, we take actions to create the new life based on our truth. We think it, we breathe it, and we live it. Our vision is finally taking shape and form, and soon we will experience a life-changing transformation that will lead to a completely different life than we had before.

Awakening into a new phase of life certainly changed the focus of my life. I was no longer driven to have a job. My life centered on sharing my story, teaching my lessons, and writing my books to inspire change. Even the pain I was causing my family didn't stop me from living my truth or fulfilling my calling. I felt that my entire life would not have any purpose unless I could speak my truth.

My inner truth is living by the essence of oneness, as I mentioned before. Every day, I am doing a little bit more to live according to my vision of oneness, such as building relationships with friends from different ethnicities and cultural backgrounds that enrich my life with great depth and wisdom. Often, I share information that emphasizes the similarities between all spiritual teachings that enhance our natural inclination to connect and be one. I love to get involved and learn about the different spiritual practices that help us connect heart to heart and have no boundaries. Being open to any styles of living is my new identity.

When people ask me, "What are you now?"

I say "Nothing," which really means that I am everything, undefined, and unlimited. Isn't that a godlike quality?

When we change ourselves and our lives, as I did, we help everyone around us realize the impact of this change—and they gradually become part of it.

We have to activate our life's mission and fight for our truth. Sometimes it involves huge risks that jeopardize lives since the message is so controversial and before its time, even though the change is already in the making. Personally, I think that our truth is always aligned with the trend of our time. For instance, the concept of oneness expressed through my spiritual teaching and many contemporary scholars is only one aspect of the trend of oneness that is being formulated in our time. This universal trend also manifested financially through the European Union market, which was established in 1993. It was empowered even more so by the

Internet that connected and built relationships of people all over the world. The Universe is helping us to create a new trend in history as we all become one.

No matter what the truth was, the truth needed to be told. Even those who took the lives of renowned visionaries, such as Mahatma Gandhi and Martin Luther King, couldn't stop them from speaking their truth. They died fighting for their truth, but their deaths didn't put an end to their vision; it only enhanced it. In spite of the force resistance, the change is inevitable and leads to improvement.

When we change and live by our truth, we are able to inspire a global change.

A starter to implement the teaching of rebirth:
- Live an awakened life, living your truth every day of your life.
- Believe in your own ability to change the world simply by living your truth.
- Create the world in your own spiritual image.

CHAPTER 7

MISSION: KARMA AND AWAKENING OF EMPATHY

It is through weakness and vulnerability that most of us learn empathy and compassion and discover our soul.
~ Bishop Desmond Tutu

The meaning of the word "Karma," known in Sanskrit as *Kamma*, is "action" based on the law of cause and effect. The belief in *karma*, related to the process of reincarnation in Hinduism, indicates that the soul comes back to an earthly life to work on the *karmic* debt it accumulated in previous lifetimes. According to the Hindu tradition, negative *karma* delays the spiritual progression of the soul, which brings the soul back in time to a lower caste that is less privileged. Positive *karma* progresses the soul forward to the next level, rewarding it with a better life. I assume that a person who serves his own interest without any consideration of others, accumulates negative *karma*. And positive *karma* accumulates when a person uses his talents and efforts to serve others.

Contrary to the Hindu tradition, I tend to believe that *karma* is not a deserving destiny based on previous lifetimes but rather is comprised of pressing life lessons that hold the key to personal and global transformation.

Each lifetime, we learn a valuable lesson that helps us to develop awareness to a universal problem. By facing our own pain and challenges, we develop empathy toward the pain that other people experience. Empathy is a powerful feeling that opens our hearts and motivates us to offer help to the one who is suffering. It indicates a turning point when the student learns his or her lesson and becomes a teacher who teaches the path of triumph. Only when we use our wisdom and knowledge to benefit society, we are able to thrive from the satisfaction of giving back.

This is what the Masters were able to achieve, by living and speaking their truth. Each truth was different, since it was subjective to the experiences they each had, but the process was similar. The Masters were inspired by an awakening of empathy, which catalyzed them to embark on their respective journeys to seek their truth to create the outcome they longed for. In the first chapter of their lives, they were students learning lessons and overcoming challenges. Later on, they became teachers, using the knowledge and skills they had gained, to offer new and often radical solutions to old, seemingly intractable problems.

In this chapter, I will focus on the direct *karmic* experiences of the Masters, which invoked their awakening of empathy and reshaped their ethos. The empathic lessons they learned from their life experiences laid the foundation for the formation of the Golden Rule.

Step 7: Mission

Buddha:
The Sufferer who Turned into a Liberator

Buddha learned from his own experiences about the pain of survival and the pain of attachment that held spiritual development back. This truly helped him to see people's misery and relate to their situation. It also made him realize that suffering is an integral part of life.

In spite of the bumpy road, Gautama successfully reached the everlasting peace he had wished for and was eager to share his wisdom with people who needed it. He recognized the importance of his mission to stop suffering altogether, but he was not confident in his ability to teach it.

Maybe it is too complicated, maybe I am not the right person...who would listen? he asked.

His fears undermined his confidence.

Feelings of confusion almost stopped Gautama from delivering his mission. He was worried that his teachings would be too complicated to understand, and he was unsure how to summarize it. "If I taught the Dhamma, people would not understand it and that would be exhausting and disappointing to me."[1]

The Brahman God was very disappointed in Buddha's hesitation and pleaded with him to change his mind because people needed his wisdom. Not everyone would understand his teachings, but those who were ready for them would be. "Lord, please preach the Dahmma...there are people with only a little desire left within them who are pining for lack of this method; some of them will understand it."[2]

This dialogue was another form of inner communication; Buddha felt empathy toward the people who suffered and had no help. He couldn't end the journey of seeking a cure for suffering.

What's the point of finding a cure for suffering, if no one would benefit from it? he asked.

The idea that people would continue to suffer frustrated him even more. This, I believe, was the inspiration of the Golden Rule, which is, according to Buddha: "Hurt not others in ways that you yourself would find hurtful."[3]

When Buddha had resolved his inner conflict, he was ready to start his mission as a teacher. The Buddha's teaching is called the:
"Noble Eightfold Path."

First Path: "Right View"

Gautama learned about the objective picture of life after he had left the collective "truth" found in the palace where he had been brought up. He realized the solution to a problem must come from the problem itself. He arrived at this conclusion simply through his own journey. One must identify the objective truth, which always includes a dark side; without it, one would not be motivated to seek the light.[4]

Second Path: "Right Thinking"

Gautama was well aware of his fear of an unknown future and the emotional blocks he had. He spent many hours thinking about the pain he had caused his family. When life was hard, he missed his old life. This yearning for the security of the past certainly increased his fear of his unknown future. Gautama lost valuable time to the fear that slowed him down. He summarized his conclusion, claiming that a "right thought" should focus on a present situation, leading to an action. It is the opposite of an empathy thought, which focuses on negative feelings such as fear of the future, or dwelling on disappointments of the past.[5]

Third Path: "Right Mindfulness"

The struggle of attachment was the toughest issue that Gautama faced. He had to let go of his old life. He had to give up his old identity completely, knowing that he would never again be a prince, and he would never again see his family. Gautama knew that giving up his old life would focus him on his goal. He must stay on task; he must commit his time completely to pursuing his heart's desire. This is the meaning of mindfulness, where one must focus energy on the here and now, not on should, could, and would.[6] When one is looking at oneself in the present, one is able to exchange habits for those that will serve them better.[7]

Fourth Path: "Right Livelihood"

Gautama's life in the past had nourished his egoistic needs, which focused his actions on himself. Gautama enjoyed his popularity and his wealth, but his life was empty and meaningless. His struggle in the forest gave him a purpose: to fight suffering and proffer solutions. Gautama advised people to find an occupation based on love and compassion; one that serves people and makes the world a better place.[8]

Fifth Path: "Right Speech"

The road to redemption is long and complicated. Gautama had many encounters with Mara, which taught him to control his ego. Therefore, he advised that we must find positive speech to communicate with the people around us, even the people we are in conflict with, in order to create harmonious surroundings.[9] Gautama proved that inner power is much more powerful then the power of ego.

Sixth Path: "Right Action"

Gautama's personal liberation gave him the motivation to be a messenger of change, offering his love and compassion to make a difference in people's lives. Gautama believed that any act of service should be based on love and compassion.[10]

Seventh path: "Right Effort"

Gautama looked back on his life, realizing that his intense practice of self-control had been a mistake. He arrived at the conclusion that too much effort is frustrating, and a lack of effort, as he experienced from his life as a prince, delays the soul's progression. Gautama encouraged people to make a basic effort to incorporate love and compassion in their daily lives, until it became second nature.[11]

Eighth Path: "Right Concentration"

Just as Gautama learned that too much effort blocks progress, he learned that awareness promotes progression. Gautama always listened to his inner voice; it guided him forward in his journey. He encouraged people to develop awareness, and to acknowledge when doors were closing in one direction and opening in another. Pay attention![12]

Gautama's life experiences were the foundations of his teachings. He went back to his five companions in Deer Park to tell them the news. These gods gave Gautama their blessing. They were thrilled that Gautama was going on a mission to cure the world of its suffering. They said, "The Lord has set the Wheel of Dhamma in motion in the Deer Park of Varanasi!"[13]

Buddha, The Enlightened One, finally came to peace with his mission to teach the *Dharma*. He traveled with his monks and taught ways to transcend suffering. He showed compassion, comforted, healed sick, trained monks, counseled kings, and advocated for social and legal reform. The order of the Sangha he established was responsible for the pursuit of individual enlightenment and salvation of humanity through meditation study and *Dharma* teaching.

Step 7: Mission

Moses:
The Refugee who Became a Leader of the Refugees

Moses was a refugee who saved himself from the stress of living against his truth that he experienced from his life in Egypt. In Midian, Moses reconstructed his life among people of peace who respected one another. This transition made an impact on Moses' life, learning a different model of leadership, which inspired him to become a leader.

Moses' escape from the stressful life in Egypt made him contemplate the possible redemption of the slaves who suffered from similar humiliation under the cruel leadership of the pharaoh.

Here, in the desert, they would be able to reconstruct their lives as I did; they would be as free and as safe as I am, he thought.

What was impossible in Egypt could be possible in the desert. Moses realized that his own process of redemption, which began when he had started a new chapter of his life in Midian, had given him confidence and a solution he had never found before.

The desert was a large land where many small tribes lived in harmony. *There is room for more people on this land, he thought.*

I think that Moses envisioned in his mind how here, in this free territory, he could establish a new nation based on the principle of law that he would help enforce with love and respect. This goal filled Moses with excitement about living his truth and changing the lives of many people who needed his help.

Now that Moses found a place, he had to plan the process of liberation so he could bring the slaves to freedom and peace. Moses began preparing the Hebrews to leave Egypt in the middle of the night, just as he had, and bringing them to the desert in order to create a new nation committed to law and justice—the antithesis of the corrupt state of the Egyptian regime.

Moses' own lesson as a refugee who escaped discrimination motivated him to repeat this cycle in order to bring the refugees to freedom. This cycle is known in Hebrew as "Tikkun Olam," and translates to correction, or "repairing the world," which is parallel to *karma*. Through the process of reaching out to help others, we heal our own pain.

It is this *karma* that transformed and changed Moses' life. His liberation was not complete until he had used his knowledge and the lessons of his own experience to repair the life that he had escaped from. Only then would Moses be free and content.

Moses' *karmic* cycle, from a refugee, who had escaped chaos, to a leader of the refugees, was based on the awakening of empathy. Moses knew pain and stress firsthand from his experiences in Egypt. As he helped others, he was liberated from the same pain he had experienced in the past. He finally was healing the scar in his own soul.

The awakening of empathy is the foundation of the Golden Rule, which was established in Judaism by the middle-aged Rabbi Hillel even though it was inspired by Moses' awakening of empathy.

Before sharing the story about the Golden Rule, I should explain that the Jewish people in the middle age years, who came to seek advice from their respectful rabbis, chose between two popular approaches: the House of Shammai, who was strict in their ruling, and the House of Hillel, which was known for offering a doable and reasonable solution. The story of the Golden Rule tells us about a gentile who considered conversion; he was seeking advice about the knowledge of the Torah, which was required for the purpose of converting.

A certain heathen came to Shammai and said to him, "Make me proselyte, on one condition that you teach me the whole Torah while I stand on one foot." Thereupon he repulsed him with a rod, which was in his hand. When he went to Hillel, he said to him, "What is hateful to you, do not do to your fellow; that is the whole Torah; all the rest of it is commentary; go and learn."[14]

This story summarizes the essence of the Torah, a book of the original Jewish law which Moses was its founder.

Although Rabbi Hillel was the one who established the Golden Rule in Judaism: "What is hateful to you, do not do to your fellow,"[15]—it was Moses who established the Jewish law.

I believe that the Golden Rule was inspired by the lesson that Moses had learned as he redeemed himself from the oppressive regime in Egypt, and which he redeemed once again when he established a new society based on law. Moses taught his people the empathic connection when he established a new law: "You shall not wrong a stranger or oppress him, for you were strangers in the land of Egypt."[16]

The Golden Rule conveys the empathic directive to avoid harmful acts toward others. Moses' law teaches people to avoid harmful behavior through a series of "Do not do" mitzvoth, which he established first in the Ten Commandments. The believers learned what they should not do, such as, "You shall not kill, you shall not commit adultery, and you shall not steal."[20]

These mitzvoth, or obligations, focus on what a person should not do, but they don't teach a person what he or she should do to be a better person. This is formulated through *karmic* lessons and the awakening of empathy, and is subjective, according to the lessons each person must learn.

In every lifetime, the soul completes tasks that were unaccomplished before, focusing on one of the three levels of *Tikkun* (which is a word of Kabbalah meaning repairing one soul through the process of reincarnation): "As long as a person is unsuccessful in his purpose in this world, the Holy one, blessed be He, uproots him and replants him over and over again."[18]

This is paralleled to the description in the book of Job, where we learn about the process of reincarnation, which occurs several times in order to redeem *karma*, which leads to liberation from the impact of ego-driven actions.[19]

Like the Hindu and the Buddhist traditions that teach about reincarnation, a mystical branch of Judaism called Kabbalah, indicates there is a similar process which claims that people are not capable of total transformation in just one lifetime. We must better ourselves through the process of reincarnation, fulfilling the three levels of spiritual progression over time: the Nefesh/Id; the Ruach/Ego; and the Neshamah/Super Ego. These words in Hebrew are parallel in meaning to the definition Freud had given to understand the soul's structure.[20] Without getting too much into it, the Kabbalah indicates the soul progressing through it. Each lifetime, the soul accomplishes the assignment of *karma* that focuses on one of these three aspects.

The Nefesh (soul) is the lower level of the soul and is focused on the mitzvoth that relates to function and pleasure (Id), such as reproduction, the ingestion of food, and so on.

Ruach is the emotional essence of the soul, focused on the social aspect of the Mitzvoth, which teaches self-control and discipline to control the ego. These mitzvoth include the Ten Commandments: Do not lie, do not kill, and so on.

Neshamah is the higher level of the soul, where one uses one's talents to benefit others, by doing "Gemilut Chasidim," reaching out to help people.[21]

The ultimate goal is to reach the highest level, which is focused on fulfilling the spiritual truth of the soul, as Moses did. A soul that reaches this level is no longer possessed by ego. It has attained the highest level of spirituality, which is to serve. The soul returns to God after it fulfills its spiritual purpose.[22] This process is very similar to the union of the soul with the higher God, Brahman, according to the Hindu tradition.

Moses accomplished the third level of *karma* when he dedicated his life to public work. He began to establish laws three months after freeing the slaves from Egypt. He gathered the people of Israel in a big assembly where he pronounced them as the nation of Israel and their commitment to God: "Now then, if you will obey Me faithfully and keep My covenant, you shall be My treasured possession among all the peoples."[23]

The formal covenant with the Israelites required a commitment from each person who strives to act upon God's law as given by Moses. Moses continued to establish laws during their stay in the desert; he paid special attention to justice and human rights, hoping to treat all creatures fairly regardless of their position. He ruled that everyone deserved a day of rest to recharge and enjoy the fruits of their labor. In this he included cattle, slaves, and foreigners: "Six days you shall labor and do all your work, but the seventh day is a sabbath of the Lord your God: you shall not do any work—you, and your son or daughter, your male or female slave, or your cattle, or the stranger who is within your settlements."[24]

Moses was especially attentive toward the weak who couldn't defend themselves. He wished to protect slaves from being used and humiliated, as they had been in Egypt, by limiting a slave's commitment to his master to a six-year period; in the seventh year, the slave would be set free without money.[25]

Moses also tried to prevent discrimination and abuse. The law must protect the financial rights of those who couldn't provide for themselves, such as widows, orphans, and foreigners. He was determined to ensure that people treated them with fairness and respect: "You shall not subvert the rights of the stranger or the fatherless; you shall not take a widow's garment in pawn."[26]

The law required avoiding profit of interest when giving a loan to poor people, those who one were supposed to help and not take advantage of. "If you lend money to my people, to the poor among you, do not act toward them as a creditor; exact no interest from them."[27]

These laws were based on common sense and, if adhered to, would guarantee a highly functional society. Moses had started the process, but Jewish law would be completed in the year 220 CE with redacting of the Mishnah (the Oral Law).

Step 7: Mission

Jesus:
A Teacher of Selflessness

E ven though Jesus was an observant Jew following the Jewish law, he strongly believed that people must act leniently to compensate for the severity of the Jewish system of justice. In some cases the Jewish law fails to treat moral issues at the roots. Jesus longed for a reformation of Jewish law that would address those issues.

Fearing resistance to his truth, Jesus took time off to think things through. It was at this point that he spent forty days in the wilderness engaging in an inner conflict with the Devil, wherein he was tempted as we have discussed earlier in this book.[28]

Only a man who had dealt with the temptations of the ego himself would be capable of helping the "tempters of the ego" overcome their own challenges: "For since he himself has passed through the test of suffering, he is able to help those who are meeting their test now."[29]

The Devil promised Jesus social popularity, economic bounty, and an honorable position in his community to empower his ego. Yet, committing to fame, popularity, and money is like worshiping the Devil who purposely diverted people's attention from their spiritual purpose. This is a common conflict that we face when we want to do more to help people, but at the same time, we must take care of our own existing needs.

Jesus rejected the Devil's offer, realizing that he would much rather worship God by fulfilling the spiritual calling. If one is worshiping himself by fulfilling only egoistic goals for the sake of being powerful, popular, and rich, one is worshiping his "inner devil." But if one is dedicating his life to service using his natural gift to create a better life, one is godlike.

Jesus clearly stated this, based on his own experience: "No servant can be the slave of two masters...."[30] If you are motivated by ego, you will live your life satisfying your own needs throughout your lifetime. But if you are motivated by the conscience of service, you live a meaningful life to serve others and leave a legacy through your divine power.

The *karmic* connection from the lesson that Jesus learned gave him the motivation and the knowledge to teach this exact message to those people whose egos dominated their behavior. Jesus understood their temptation and the mindset that led to such behavior. He had time to think about the implications of forgiveness while staying in the desert. He studied the Torah all his life, learning about self-improvement and morality, but understanding the *karmic* connection between the lesson one must learn and the mission of teaching what one teaches was a pivotal moment.

Jesus returned to Galilee after he resolved his own inner conflicts and started his mission without any further hesitation. According to the Book of Luke in the New Testament, Jesus first revealed his mission to the public in the synagogue, when he quoted from the scroll of the prophet Isaiah, in a passage concerning redemption and the coming of a redeemer: "The spirit of the Lord is upon me because he has anointed me; he has sent me to announce good news to the poor, to proclaim release for prisoners and recovering of the sight of the blind; to let the broken victims go free, to proclaim the year of the Lord's favour."[31]

"Today," he said, "In your very hearing this text has come true."[32]

Jesus tried to convince the public that he had discovered a new way to improve the quality of life. He revealed his revolutionary concept in one sentence that summed up his entire teaching: "Love your neighbor as yourself"[34] in addition to the Ten Commandments.

The Golden Rule, as Jesus summarized it, is founded on the awakening of empathy. The Golden Rule by implication suggests that we each have an obligation to teach others how to overcome their own challenges, through the insight we gain from our own journey of suffering. If we love people, we can't let them suffer the same way. Love and compassion toward someone who suffers is the motivation to fulfill our life's purpose.

Jesus claimed that he came to complete the Jewish law and elevate it to a higher level of morality. The Jewish law was formulated by the "Do not do" list of mitzvoth, which defined the boundaries between permitted actions and forbidden actions. The Ten Commandments determined the basic prohibitions for a functional society:

> "You shall not commit murder;
> You shall not commit adultery;
> You shall not steal;
> You shall not give false evidence against your neighbor;
> You shall not covet your neighbor's house; you shall not covet your neighbor's wife, his slave…or anything that belongs to him."[34]

Jesus wished to establish a new approach that would focus on the act of doing and giving to replace the "do not do" concept with a different mindset of "do more." Avoiding intentional harm was common sense, a basic level of morality in the time of Moses in 1391 BCE. But people in the first century were capable of advancing their morality. They needed to open their hands with their hearts.

The Golden Rule of Christianity, "Do onto other as you would have them do to you,"[35] gives people the freedom to do the maximum they can possibly do to help another human being in need. The Golden Rule in Judaism, "What is hateful to you, do not do to your fellow,"[36] minimized the rule to a list of actions to avoid, and limited believers' actions to an exact number of 613 mitzvoth as their duty to God. But Jesus encouraged people to do more than they could, walk that extra mile, in order to improve the quality of life for everyone.

Both the Jewish approach and Jesus' point of view are equally essential. It is important to demonstrate self-control and discipline, which keeps us from hurting other human beings. And it is important to be kind and generous to others. These two directives complete each other.

Yet, Jesus' teaching was not focused on behavior, but rather on a vision. He wished to create a non-egoistic society in which people would give their talents to improve the collective quality of life, the same way that Jesus used his gift of healing to help people. Every person has a unique truth, and everyone has something valuable to give and contribute. By doing what we do best, we leave our spiritual marks on the world, and the world is better because of it.

In his speeches, Jesus articulated many examples that illustrated his vision of a better life: "When a man takes your coat, let him have your shirt as well; when a man takes what is yours, do not demand it back. Treat others as you would like them to treat you."[37]

Jesus called upon the public to love their enemies, referring to the sinners who were condemned and separated from the public because of their erroneous behavior. At that time, the general public was not allowed to interact with sinners, which caused a social split among families. Jesus wished to change the punitive nature of the criminal justice system. Instead, he offered compassion, according to which the sinners would be able to reconstruct their lives. "Love your enemies; do good to those who hate you; bless those who curse you; pray for those who treat you spitefully."[38]

Jesus himself was not afraid to interact with sinners. He broke the norm when he ate with them, causing the respected members of the Pharisees to question his choices: "It is not the healthy that need a doctor, but the sick..."[39] he answered them.

Jesus believed that all sinners deserved a chance to learn from their errors. In fact, this path is probably more powerful than the safer path of righteousness that doesn't provide enough challenges for development and growth: "...I tell you, there will be greater joy in heaven over one sinner who repents than over ninety-nine righteous people who do not need to repent."[40]

Jesus deeply disagreed with the Jewish idea of justice summarized through the expression: "Eye for eye, tooth for tooth,"[41] which ironically is not an original Jewish concept. It was influenced by the civil law that had been established by King Hammurabi from Babylonia in 1790 BCE.

Accordingly, justice could only be achieved through a punitive system. But in reality, this concept encourages resentment and revenge. Making the sinner pay for his mistakes gives the victim a sense of victory, but it doesn't resolve the situation. The sinner committing the crime feels resentment rather than remorse. Instead, Jesus offered the policy of forgiveness and peace: "Do not set yourself against the man who wrongs you, if someone slaps you on the right cheek, turn and offer him your left."[42]

A true solution is based on forgiveness. If the victim could forgive the sinner, he would be able to leave it in the past and move on with his life. He could allow the sinner to express remorse and change his life for the better so he would not repeat his mistakes. This way, both sides would be able to move on with their lives and no resentment would affect their futures.

Jesus dedicated his life to building a foundation for a new life where people would be motivated by the essence of love and compassion. He didn't want to reconstruct the "broken pieces" with external fixes; he wished to uproot the old foundation and replace it with one that was intrinsically solid. To his way of thinking, if people could reprogram their pattern of thinking, they might be able to embrace this progressive idea of change. Jesus' actions demonstrate the exact same spiritual principal that we become aware of today—when we are replacing one thought with another we are able to create a total shift.

Step 7: Mission

Muhammad:
The Orphan who Protected the Weak

Muhammad arrived in Medina, where he established his vision, in 622 CE. Initially Muhammad brought the Muslim immigrants from Mecca and Abyssinia to practice the Islamic faith freely, in peace. The Umma community that Muhammad created in Medina was based on religion and not on kinship, as it had been. To become a member, his followers had to make *hajira* to leave their tribe in order to join the Umma. One of its precepts was that no Muslim would fight against another, no matter what tribe they came from: "Those who believed and made the *hajira* and struggled with possessions and persons in the way of God and those who gave their homes and 'helped' these are *awliya* protectors of one another..."[43]

Muhammad made a covenant of mutual obligation among all his followers and the Jews of the oasis, forming a single community united against pagans, which was also a tactical move.

Muhammad continued his teaching in Medina, and soon the clans of Aws and the Khazraj had converted to Islam. Muhammad instituted the brotherhood between the helpers (the locals) and the emigrants, in order to unite the community of believers and strengthen it.

Muhammad stopped their fighting and spoke to their hearts: "O Muslim," he said, and then twice pronounced the Divine Name, *Allah Allah,* "Will ye act," he went on, "as in the days of Ignorance, what though I am with you, and God hath guided you onto Islam, and honored you with it, and thereby enable you to break with pagan ways, and thereby saved you from disbelief, and thereby united your heart? At once they realized that they had led astray, and they wept, and embraced each other and returned with the Prophet to the city, attentive and obedient to his words"[44]

Muhammad captured people's trust with his passion, and he demonstrated great skills of leadership, both spiritually and politically.

Muhammad had been motivated by his own *karmic* lesson to care for people in need, and he emphasized that every member of the community had a responsibility to protect every other member of the community, to offer protection during times of war, and to otherwise insure the common welfare at all times. The Golden Rule established by Muhammad clearly stated that helping one another is the foundation of the faith of Islam: "Not one of you is a believer until he desire for his brother what he desire for himself."[45]

Muhammad's own *karmic* lesson from his old life back in Mecca had inspired this Golden Rule: he was an orphan child raised by family members from a young age, losing his mother when was just six years old and his grandfather at eight, and his family was poor and belonged to the weaker clan of the Hashim, of the tribe of the Quraysh. Muhammad remembered how his relatives took care of him, and he always was grateful for their kindness. Since then, he paid attention to people in need, and he had witnessed many family members struggle to provide food for their families. He knew firsthand how difficult it was to be poor and neglected while other people in the tribe enjoyed a luxurious lifestyle. Muhammad was lucky enough to be able to help his family members ease their financial burden, given that he eventually married a wealthy widow and made a good living. But he was frustrated that he couldn't help everyone in need and was disappointed that most people turned a blind eye to those who needed help the most.

Muhammad was attracted to monotheism primarily due to its fundamental tenet that God had created the world in perfect balance. If people would submit themselves to God's will, they would fulfill His wish and obey His laws: "Whoever submits himself entirely to Allah and he is the doer of good to others, he had his reward from his Lord and there is no fear for such nor shall they grieve."[46]

Islam was founded on the concept of submission to God's will, which gives Islam its name. Its followers are obliged to be responsible to all members of the community, thereby bridging the gap between weak and strong and removing obstacles to harmonious living. By taking responsibility in this manner, the believers of Islam would maintain the divine balance that had been created by God.

Later on, Muhammad established the policy of *zakat,* according to which believers must give a portion of their income to the community.[47]

Distributing wealth equally between the members strengthened the community in general, but it also helped to balance the egos of the wealthy and kept them somewhat humble. The community of Umma that Muhammad established in Medina was founded on egalitarian principles, requiring dues from everyone (some through pay, some through work) in order to avoid becoming an elitist society.[48] Alms-giving bridged the gap between rich and poor and helped the slaves to achieve emancipation;

it became one of the five essential pillars of Islam among payer, fasting, pilgrimage to Mecca, and the faith in one God.

Muhammad told his followers about the concept of the afterlife, wherein they would return to God's world in heaven. Such a concept was revolutionary to the pagan Arabs, but it was in accordance with the notion of an individual's responsibility to keep or restore God's balance. Given the supposition of an afterlife, Muhammad encouraged his people to do good works beyond the giving of alms, for he believed that all charitable acts would be accounted for in the court of God and that each person would ultimately be judged on the merits of their charitable acts. Everything depended on individuals' actions in their lifetimes. If they did their best to obey God's law and live by God's wishes, they would be rewarded in the next world. If they disobeyed God's wishes and undermined God's order, they would have to pay for their actions.

Either way, they would be returning to face God's judgment. Muhammad developed the concept of "Return" through a direct revelation from the angel Gabriel, which most likely was inspired by the afterlife concept in both Judaism and Christianity. In any event, Muhammad made the adjustment to fit Islam's spirit.

Islam is a faith of justice. Muhammad wished to protect the weak, especially the orphans and widows who had lost their men in battle defending Islam. He asked men to marry widows, and he encouraged polygamy to protect the poor widows and their children:

"Give orphans their property, do not replace their good things with bad; and do not consume their property with your own-a great sin. If you fear that you will not deal fairly with orphan girls, you may marry whichever other women seem good to you, two, three, or four. If you fear you cannot be equitable to them, then marry only one or your slave right, that is more likely to make you avoid Bias."[49]

Once again, Muhammad issued a call to do the right thing: to give women and children a chance to rebuild their lives after having suffered an almost irreparable loss, otherwise their lives might be spent in utter destitution. Muhammad also fought against the cycle of revenge; he called to replace it with the concept of blood-money: a monetary fine imposed on one who had taken a life or had committed an equally serious transgression (as opposed to the "life for a life" mandate that is part of the old tradition in Arabia).[50]

These were all progressive and far-reaching measures, which formulate the new nation of Islam.

The Spiritual Lesson of Mission

A s we gleaned from the Masters, the awakening of empathy is, in a large part, activated by the life challenges we personally experience. First we experience the pain of suffering in order to understand the weakness and dysfunctional situation inside and out, and then we overcome it with our own determination.

Our own pain motivates us to be compassionate beings first and foremost. When we overcome our own challenges, we teach others the lessons we learned, and to do our part to resolve the collective pain and struggles. By helping others, we heal our own scars and release Karmic debt. The Karmic lesson helps us to progress to a higher level—liberated from ego, so we can reach out to others and shine our light for all to see.

Although reincarnation has never been substantiated by science, it was discovered and acknowledged by hypnotherapists (such as Dr. Brian Weiss, who is best known for his reincarnation research) through elaborate processes of investigation.

Another known hypnotherapist is Dr. Michael Newton, the author of *Journey of Souls,* who focuses his research on collecting evidence from his clients about the transition between lives. Unlike the common belief that souls face God's judgment as they return home, he described a peaceful and loving heaven as though souls relax from their hard labor on Earth. During the temporary stay in heaven, between lives, souls learn and evaluate the spiritual progress that they achieved in their previous lifetime.[51]

This reincarnation process is like going from one grade to another. Each grade teaches the souls new skills that can be used in their next lifetime. Therefore, souls are constantly improving and progressing (in spite of the Hindu claims that souls can progress and regress). Being a schoolteacher myself, I believe that even a weak student learns something during his stay in school. Some souls might progress slowly, repeating more "school years" (more lifetimes), but they are moving forward nevertheless.

Dr. Newton categorized souls as beginner souls or advance souls, depending upon their learning experience in their previous lifetimes. Beginner souls are dependable characters who tend to strive for structure and organized lifestyles to provide stability in their lives.[52] Their *karmic* lesson will focus on tasks that teach them skills of responsibility and independence. They also will face behavioral issues to teach them self-control and motivate them to change. I tend to believe that Beginner souls progress slowly but surely through many lifetimes. A soul that doesn't achieve its goal will return to earth with an easier task—so it experiences success—instead of a harder one to punish it.

Intermediate souls are independent; their behavior is controlled as they reacquire skills from their previous lifetimes.[53] These souls experience more complex challenges in fewer lifetimes to increase the potential of evolution.[54] These progressive souls fight to break the traditional structure, improving quality of life and paving the way for change. I am not an expert on the subject but I believe that a soul like Helen Keller (1880-1968) is a perfect example to illustrate it because she was born blind and deaf. In spite of her physical limitations, Keller was able to develop a new way to communicate. She pursued a higher education and wrote many books to educate people about the unlimited abilities of handicapped people. Her disability served as a motivation to raise public awareness; others found ways to help individuals with similar problems.[55]

Advanced souls are unusually kind and compassionate people. Their ability to deal with challenges is unbelievably strong since they have done it so many times before. Advanced souls come to earth to change consciousness and heal the world.[56] Their *karmic* lesson is focused on a shifting of global consciousness, such as the Masters did. They dedicate their lives to helping people and fighting injustice in order to change and improve life. Even though these souls are very powerful, they frequently prefer a simple life. Lack of selfish desire allows them to focus on what matters most, which is their spiritual mission.

I hope you would agree that Gandhi (1869-1948) is an example of such a soul. Gandhi was well-known in the world as a man who "fought" for justice and peace. He arrived in Africa as a young lawyer and worked there for one year in 1893. In Africa, Gandhi experienced discrimination firsthand because of his Indian roots, and he decided to stay and fight the law that forbade voting by the Indian minority. He also offered free legal advice to people suffering discrimination. In 1915, he returned to India to lead the non-violent war of independence through public assemblies and quiet protest. Gandhi taught the public that non-violent actions can be very successful in achieving long-term goals. His simplicity commanded unusual power, and the importance of his mandate remains unmatched today: "Be the change you wish to see in the world."[57]

From all of these examples we learn that we are here to serve. Initially we overcome the challenge of our own karmic lesson, through which we develop empathy to help people who are suffering from a similar challenge.

When we change, we pave the way for a new direction; we set up an invigorated pattern that replaces the old, dysfunctional one. This is as essential today as it was in the time of Moses, Buddha, Muhammad, and Jesus.

A starter to implement the teaching of awakening of empathy:

- Identify the pain you endured throughout your life and think about what you have to offer for those who suffer from it.
- Answer: Who needs your help? What audience will best benefit from your message?
- Plan how to reach out to people who need your wisdom.

Epilogue

Climbing to a Higher Level of Consciousness

The godlike journey as demonstrated through the Masters' lives shows the evolution of the soul in one lifetime from the basic level of consciousness into a higher level of consciousness. Through this process we transform from a state of survivors into a state of creators.

This process takes us through three primary levels of consciousness: seeking spiritual truth, developing awareness, and activating our divinity. In the conclusion chapter of this book, I will explain the contribution of these three primary levels of consciousness to our soul's progression.

We all have the potential to evolve through this process and master each one of the three levels of consciousness. This book's purpose is to help us develop the awareness of this journey so we could benefit from executing our divine potential and bring so much light into this world.

This book was inspired by the Masters' journeys and based on the stories from Scriptures. However, I would like to point out the great similarities between the Masters' journeys and the spiritual quest highlighted by the hero's journey defined by the late mythologist and author Joseph Campbell. Both journeys highlight the three primary levels of spiritual consciousness through their similarities and the differences.

I believe that the comparison of the two is necessary, especially since many spiritual teachings put so much attention on creation consciousness, and then ignore the prior levels of consciousness that needs to be established beforehand. It is much like the process of reading: an illiterate child or person can't read or understand Shakespearian language. The skills of reading need to be acquired first, then building a vocabulary, moving toward abstract concepts and sophisticated language. The same process is applicable to spiritual growth; we must develop a higher consciousness throughout a gradual process, facing challenges in our lives.

By putting emphasis on the journey in both cases, we become aware of the entire process that allowed us to evolve from human to divine.

The basic level of consciousness is formulating our spiritual truth through the challenges of the physical existence. The challenges we encounter are helping us to eliminate the "untruth" from our life and make better choices that bring us closer to our own truth.

Joseph Campbell called the first part of the hero journey "separation," which is normally caused by a crisis of some sort that forces a situation of leaving in order to explore the world beyond the close surroundings. This process gives people a chance to learn, adjust, and evolve. Though I agree with the outcome of separation, I tend to believe it is initiated by disagreement with the norm, expressing yearning to discover our own truth as we discussed throughout the first chapters.

When we graduate from the first part of the journey, we will have a clear idea about our spiritual truth, which helps us make conscious choices about the path of life that is right for us. Our spiritual truth helps us to seek the directions of our hearts.

The second level of consciousness is awareness, formulated by an internal process of transformation. When we start exploring life, absorbing new information, adjusting to new thinking, and adopting a new lifestyle, we become aware of a different truth that makes more sense to us. In order to reach a higher level of consciousness, we should release ourselves from the old mindset, eliminating everything that does not support us in our truth.

According to Campbell, the second part of the hero's journey is "initiation," as the hero deals with his challenges and learns his lesson. I believe that the greatest challenges in our lives are caused by our resistance to accept the truth because of our tendency to fulfill social expectations. If we choose to deny our truth and live by the old mindset, we are going on the wrong path that leads us to more chaos in our lives. But when we make choices to live by this newfound truth, we will be able to find our desired destination and reach enlightenment.

When we graduate from this phase, we will be able to make choices that are continually aligned with our soul truth to create harmony in our lives. We will be able to choose the people we want to share our space and vision with and eliminate those who refuse to accept our truth; we will be able to choose the place that serves and supports our essence; we will choose the lifestyle that fits it. Our life would be structured on the foundation of a newfound truth, which would allow us to find harmony and happiness.

The third and the highest level of consciousness is divinity, empowering us to create the world in our own spiritual image. The final phase, according to Campbell, is the "Return." The hero comes back home after facing his fears and overcoming his challenges. But, his real victory is the mission of teaching what he has learned, sharing his wisdom, and making a difference. This part of the journey empowers us to create and improve the world with our spiritual truth and the wisdom from the lesson we have learned.

Similarly, I believe that our divine consciousness is formulated through our journey of suffering. By going through our own pain and suffering, we become aware of the weakness and problem that many people are facing, being the eyes and the ears of those who are still suffering. As a result, we become more compassionate human beings, motivated by love to create a better world. When we finally are reaching a higher state of consciousness, we become the messenger of change, dedicated to our lives' missions. It doesn't mean that life is going to be perfect from now on and we won't face any challenges in the future, but we have the divine power to fulfill our spiritual goal because we are committed and dedicated to achieve it.

In every lifetime we work on improving our higher consciousness. We learn lessons that reduce the focus on achieving only egoistic goals in our lives, so we could develop a sense of service motivated by love and compassion.

However, the spiritual evolution of the soul does not end in one lifetime, it continues throughout many lifetimes, in which we are gradually increasing our responsibility and mission. By increasing the level of consciousness, we will be able to make much more of an impact, as we know from well-known people who contribute tremendously to the history of mankind.

We should know that we are first and foremost spiritual beings that choose to have human experience, so we can use our spiritual truth to improve human lives while we are here on earth. Therefore our life purpose is spiritual, to make a difference. We are here to create the world, using our truth and the knowledge and the wisdom that we gained from learning through our human experiences. Therefore, it is our responsibility and privilege to create what is missing, to fix a broken situation, to solve a mystery, to invent technology, to find cures to deadly diseases, and so much more.

We have all the qualities that we need to create, change, and improve life.

We should be the godlike beings that we are and leave our spiritual footprint on this world.

ACKNOWLEDGMENTS

This book has been in the making ever since I announced my liberation from Judaism in 2005. My very first intention was to define my own spiritual direction through the research and reading I have done during these past few years. My first draft of my writing was focused on what was wrong, but it evolved through the comparison of my own experiences to those of the Masters. When I first realized it, I became aware of the direction that this book was taking me. I truly believe that I was guided to write this book through divine intervention. I want to thank first and foremost the higher power that had chosen me to be a vessel and helped me to put this project into fruition.

My very first draft of this manuscript was written in my native language of Hebrew. Back then I worked with two wonderful translators, Eve E. Hecht and Michal Fram-Cohen, who both supported my dream. I learned so much from the process of translation, which helped me to build my confidence and trust myself when I became ready to write in English. My old manuscript though no longer fit the spirit of the book that I wished to write. However, I started to gain confidence in speaking and reading English fluently, mostly because of the amount of books I have been reading for this purpose. Yet writing a book in the English language seemed to be presumptuous and somehow "impossible."

And then one day I decided to try. All of a sudden the words spilled onto the paper and the flow was so smooth that I could not be stopped. I know now that English is the language of my heart, and many validation events have confirmed it. The first one had happened in my first year in the United State when I took the written driving test. I took the first test in Hebrew and failed, but I passed the English one. I don't know how it happened, but it is a true fact. I was meant to write in English, and I trust that. From that moment on, I started to write only in English, hiring my right-hand editor, Mary Ward Menke, to clean up my work. She certainly had a lot of cleaning up to do, and she is still my right hand, literally. Thank you, Mary.

When I completed my first draft of the manuscript, I felt that something was still missing. I needed to get an objective view that would help me resolve this mystery. The Universe directed me to a very talented editor, Jill Alman-Bernstein, who became my content editor. She gave me the most insightful feedback to break the manuscript down into small pieces and see it by itself. This impactful piece of advice helped me to complete the research for this book and supported the direction I had envisioned all along.

After working with Jill, I turned to my next editor, Julie Clayton, who pointed out some content questions that any objective person who is not familiar with the subject would ask. This editing brought the content and structure of the book into harmony. At this point I finally realized that I created my first book.

When I finally connected to my dear publisher, John Paul Owles, from Joshua Tree Publishing, I had a solid manuscript, but I still had more editing work to do in order to polish this work and make it sparkle. The wonderful team of editors in Joshua Tree Publishing took on this responsibility, and they did an amazing job to get to this final goal of publishing my first book. I wish to thank these editors for their contribution to finalizing the editing work. First was Mary Joy, who prepared the manuscript for editing, and then Roslyn Summerville, who had an amazing ability to see the little details. Last but not least to my wonderful publisher, John Paul, who supports and encourages me to deliver my message in spite of the challenges that I have experienced. I keep reminding myself that the tiniest light can still light up a dark room.

I want to thank each one of the editors and mentors I had mentioned above who truly had a part in my journey. I couldn't do it without each and every one of you.

Thank you for the wonderful photographer, Madeline Vite, who did the book cover shoot. Even though we can't judge a book by its cover, the cover of the book is our "first date." The cover photo is credited to Madphoto.com and thanks to Madeline Vite as the cover of the book gives us the opportunity to connect eyes to eyes and soul to soul.

A special thanks for my spiritual mentor and a dear friend, Rev. Dr. Charles Geddess, founder of Bridges of Wellness in South Florida and A Center of Spiritual Living Minster, who truly inspired me to understand the commitment of love to my spiritual calling. There were many moments that I didn't want to deliver this message, trying to protect the family I love, or I simply wished to give up. But Charles truly inspired me by example to understand that love is the only motivation to complete this difficult journey and share my message with the world. Thank you Charles for modeling the essence of love that you are truly living.

Last, but certainly not least, I want to thank my wonderful family "Mishpachat Gabay," especially my dear parents, Imma Brurya and Abbba David. They chose their life path, and I have chosen mine. The difference of beliefs and values created the distance between us, and yet, we share an amazing heart connection that will never stop enduring. Last year, when my parents came to visit in United State, I felt a sense of peace for the first time in my life. I finally realized that my family had made peace with my choices and accepted the new me. Only after I had witnessed their shift of consciousness, did I start to believe in the importance of my mission and my confidence to deliver it. I couldn't live my truth and be on this journey without my family's love and acceptance that motivates me to "Be the change I wish to see in the world."

REFERENCE NOTES:

Chapter 1

1. Huston Smith, The World's Religious, 1991, 82
2. Karen Armstrong, Buddha, New York, 2001, 30
3. Ibid., 15
4. Ibid., 31
5. John S. Strong, The Experience of Buddhism, California, 1994, 10
6. Samuel Bercholz and Sherab Chodzin Kohn, The Buddha and His Teaching, Boston, 2003, 6-7
7. John S. Strong, The Experience of Buddhism, California, 1994, 11
8. Samuel Bercholz and Sherab Chodzin Kohn, The Buddha and His Teaching, Boston, 2003, 7
9. Ibid., 8
10. Ibid.
11. Ibid.
12. Ibid., 10
13. Ibid., 8-9
14. Ibid., 11
15. Ibid.
16. Ibid.
17. Book of Legends/Sefer Ha-Aggadah: Legends from the Talmud and Midrash, by Hayyim Nuhman Bialik, Yehoshua Hana Revintzky, page 60
18. The Traditional Hebrew Text and the New JPS Translation, second Edition, 1999, Exodus1:9
19. Ibid., 1:22
20. Ibid., 2:5-6
21. Ibid., 2:10
22. Book of Legends/Sefer Ha-Aggadah: Legends from the Talmud and Midrash, by Hayyim Nuhman Bialik, Yehoshua Hana Revintzky, page 60-61

23. The Traditional Hebrew Text and the New JPS Translation, second Edition, 1999, Exodus 2:11-12
24. Ibid., 2:12
25. Ibid., 2:13
26. Ibid., 2:15
27. The New English Bible, Oxford University Press, Cambridge University Press, 1970, Luke 1:26-33
28. Ibid., Matthew 2:2-3
29. Ibid., 2:19-20
30. Harold Rosen, Founders of Faith, the Parallel Lives of God Messengers, IL 2010, 244
31. The New English Bible, Oxford University Press, Cambridge University Press, 1970, Mark 1:22
32. Ibid., 6:2-3
33. Ibid., Matthew 9:13
34. The Jesus Dynasty: The Hidden History of Jesus, His Royal Family, and the Birth of Christianity, Simon & Schuster, James Tabor, 2006, 134-135
35. Ibid., 119
36. Ibid., 121
37. The New English Bible, Oxford University Press, Cambridge University Press, 1970, Mark 5:35-42
38. THE HOLY BIBLE, NEW INTERNATIONAL VERSION®, NIV® Copyright © 1973, 1978, 1984, 2011 by Biblica, Inc.®
39. Karen Armstrong, Muhammad-a biography of the prophet, New York, 1993, 75-76
40. The New English Bible, Oxford University Press, Cambridge University Press, 1970, Luke 1:28-38
41. Exodus 2:2
42. Karen Armstrong, Muhammad-a biography of the prophet, New York, 1993, 75
43. Ibid., 76
44. Ibid., 77
45. Ibid., 66
46. Ibid., 79
47. Ibid., 81
48. Ibid., 105
49. Ibid., 136
50. Ibid., 142

51. Maulana Muhammad Ali, A Manual of Hadith, OH, 2001, Hadith Bukhari 83:23; 1:1
52. Karen Armstrong, Muhammad-a biography of the prophet, New York,1993, 150
53. Hadith Timidhi 39:2

Chapter 2

1. Karen Armstrong, Buddha, New York, 2001, 1-2
2. Ibid., 66
3. Samuel Bercholz and Sherab Chodzin Kohn, The Buddha and His Teaching, Boston, 2003, 12
4. F. L. Woodward, Some Saying of The Buddha according to the Pali Canon, 12-13
5. Clive Erricker, Buddhism, London, 1995, 37-38
6. Ibid., 38
7. The Traditional Hebrew Text and the New JPS Translation, second Edition, 1999, Exodus 2:11-12
8. Ibid., 2:14
9. Ibid., 2:15
10. Ibid., 2:17-18
11. The New English Bible, Oxford University Press, Cambridge University Press, 1970 Luke 2:49
12. Ibid., Matthew 5:17
13. Ibid., Mark 2:27
14. Ibid., Exodus 20:8-9
15. Ibid., Matthew 12:1-8
16. Ibid., Luke 12:9-12
17. Karen Armstrong, Muhammad-a biography of the prophet, New York, 1993, 77
18. Ibid., 78
19. Ibid., 79-80
20. Martine Lings, Muhammad, His Life Based on the Earliest Sources, VT, 1983, 38-39
21. Karen Armstrong, Muhammad-a biography of the prophet, New York, 1993, 58-59
22. Martine Lings, Muhammad, His Life Based on the Earliest Sources, VT, 1983, 66

23. Karen Armstrong, Muhammad-a biography of the prophet, New York, 1993, 102-103
24. Ibid., 105-106
25. Ibid., 119
26. Ibid.
27. Ibid., 119-120
28. Hadith of Bukhari, quoted in Harold Rosen, Founders of Faith, the Parallel Lives of God messengers, IL 2010, 313

Chapter 3

1. Samuel Bercholz and Sherab Chodzin Kohn, The Buddha and His Teaching, Boston, 2003, 12
2. Ibid.
3. Karen Armstrong, Buddha, New York, 2001, 44
4. Ibid., 46
5. Ibid., 101
6. W. Rahula, What the Buddha Taught, New York, 1982, 2-3
7. Karen Armstrong, Buddha, New York, 2001, 47
8. Ibid., 50-51
9. Ibid., 54-55
10. Ibid., 56
11. Ibid., 58-60
12. Ibid., 61
13. Ibid., 62
14. The Traditional Hebrew Text and the New JPS Translation, second Edition, 1999, Exodus 2:16-20
15. Ibid., Exodus 3:1
16. Ibid., Exodus 18:17-23
17. Ibid., 18:1-6
18. Ibid., 18:13
19. Ibid., 18:17-18
20. Ibid., 18: 21-23
21. The Jesus Dynasty: The Hidden History of Jesus, His Royal Family, and the Birth of Christianity, Simon & Schuster James Tabor, 2006, 128
22. The New English Bible, Oxford University Press, Cambridge University Press, Matthew 3:1-13

23. Harold Rosen, Founders of Faith, the Parallel Lives of God messengers, IL 2010, 244

24. The Jesus Dynasty: The Hidden History of Jesus, His Royal Family, and the Birth of Christianity, Simon & Schuster, James Tabor, 2006, 129

25. Ibid., 144-148

26. The New English Bible, Oxford University Press, Cambridge University Press, Matthew 3:2

27. Ibid., Luke 3:10-11

28. Ibid., Matt 3:16-17

29. Ibid., Exodus 22:25

30. Ibid., Matthew 5:41

31. Ibid., Matthew 5:40

32. The Jesus Dynasty: The Hidden History of Jesus, His Royal Family, and the Birth of Christianity, Simon & Schuster, James Tabor, 2006, 138

33. Ibid., 134

34. Ibid., 150

35. Ibid., 154

36. The New English Bible, Oxford University Press, Cambridge University Press, Luke 17:20-21

37. Karen Armstrong, Muhammad-a biography of the prophet, New York, 1993, 66-67

38. Ibid., 92-93

39. Ibid., 94-95

40. Ibid., 70

41. Ibid., 60

42. Ibid., 59

43. Ibid., 83

44. The Quran, Oxford University Press, NY, 2004 translation by M.A.S. Abdel Haleem, Sura 2:177

45. Maulana Muhammad Ali, A Munual of Hadith, OH, 2001, 169

46. The Quran, Oxford University Press, NY, 2004 translation by M.A.S. Abdel Haleem, Sura 9:21-22

Chapter 4

1. F. L. Woodward, Some Saying of The Buddha according to the Pali Canon, 1973, 12
2. John S Strong, The Experience of Buddhism, California, 1994, 15
3. Ibid.
4. .F. L. Woodward, Some Saying of The Buddha according to the Pali Canon, 1973, 13
5. Karen Armstrong, Buddha, New York, 2001, 63
6. Smith, The World's Religious, 1991, 85
7. John S Strong, The Experience of Buddhism, California, 1994, 16
8. Ibid.
9. Ibid., 17
10. Ibid.
11. Deepak Chopra, Buddha- A Story of Enlightenment, New York, 2008, 223
12. Ibid.
13. Ibid., 224
14. John S Strong, The Experience of Buddhism, California, 1994, 17
15. The Traditional Hebrew Text and the New JPS Translation, second Edition, 1999, Isaiah 2:4
16. The New English Bible, Oxford University Press, Cambridge University Press, Luke 6:35
17. Ibid., 14:12
18. Ibid., Exodus 20:9-10
19. Ibid., Matthew 12:1-7
20 Ibid., 5:17
21. Ibid.
22. Ibid., 21:5
23. Ibid., Revelation 21:4
24. Karen Armstrong, Muhammad-a biography of the prophet, New York, 1993, 58-59
25. Ibid., 96-97
26. Ibid., 82-83
27. Ibid., 85
28. Ibid., 89

29. The Quran, Oxford University Press, NY, 2004 translation by M.A.S. Abdel Haleem, Sura 93
30. Karen Armstrong, Muhammad-a biography of the prophet, New York, 1993, 85
31. Ibid.

Chapter 5

1. Karen Armstrong, Buddha, New York, 2001, 90
2. Samuel Bercholz and Kohn, The Buddha and His teaching, Boston, 2003, 15
3. Ibid.
4. Karen Armstrong, Buddha, New York, 2001, 90-91
5. Samuel Bercholz and Kohn, The Buddha and His teaching, Boston, 2003, 15
6. Karen Armstrong, Buddha, New York, 2001, 92
7. Dhammapada Commentary p. 431-432 quoted in Harold Rosen, Founders of Faith, the Parallel Lives of God messengers, IL 2010, 210
8. John S. Strong, The Experience of Buddhism, California, 1994, 17
9. Ibid.
10. Clive Erricker, Buddhism, UK, 1995, 27
11. W. Rahula, What the Buddha taught, NY, 1974, 61
12. The Traditional Hebrew Text and the New JPS Translation, second Edition, 1999, Exodus 3:2
13. Ibid., 3:3
14. Ibid., 3:2
15. Ibid., 3:4
16. Ibid.
17. The New English Bible, Oxford University Press, Cambridge University Press, 1970, Luke 2:46-47
18. Ibid., Matthew 3:16
19. Ibid., 3:2
20. The Jesus Dynasty: The Hidden History of Jesus, His Royal Family, and the Birth of Christianity, Simon & Schuster James Tabor, 2006, 138
21. Ibid., Luke 4:3
22. Ibid., 4:4

23. Ibid., 4:6-8
24. Ibid., 16:13
25. Ibid., 4:8
26. Ibid., 4:10-11
27. Ibid., 4:12
28. Ibid., Matthew 3:2
29. Ibid., 4:17
30. Maulana Muhammad Ali, A Munual of Hadith, OH, 2001, chapter 1, 2:3-5
31. Ibid., 3:14
32. Ibid., 2:7
33. Ibid.
34. Ibid.
35. Karen Armstrong, Muhammad-a biography of the prophet, New York, 1993, 84
36. Maulana Muhammad Ali, A Munual of Hadith, OH, 2001, 2:7
37. Martin Ling, Muhammad- His life Based on the Earlier Sources, 45
38. Maulana Muhammad Ali, A Munual of Hadith, OH, 2001, 2:7
39. Ibid., 2:8-9
40. Ibid., 1:2:10
41. Karen Armstrong, Muhammad-a biography of the prophet, New York, 1993, 89
42. Ibid., 89-90

Chapter 6

1. W. Rahula, What the Buddha taught, New York, 1982, p 43
2. F. L. Woodward, Some Saying of The Buddha according to the Pali Canon, 18
3. Ibid., 19
4. Karen Armstrong, Buddha, New York, 2001, 69-70
5. Ibid., 70
6. Clive Erricker, Buddhism, London, 1995, 108
7. Majjhima Nikaya 92:17-19 quoted in Harold Rosen, Founders of Faith, the Parallel Lives of God messengers, IL 2010, 228
8. Karen Armstrong, Buddha, New York, 2001, p 123: Samyutta Nikaya 22:87

9. Thich Nhat Hanh, The heart of the Buddha's teaching, New York, 1999, 156

10. The Traditional Hebrew Text and the New JPS Translation, second Edition, 1999, Exodus 3:6

11. Ibid.

12. Ibid., 33:20

13. Karen Armstrong, Muhammad-a biography of the prophet, New York, 1993, 140

14. The Traditional Hebrew Text and the New JPS Translation, second Edition, 1999, Exodus, 3:13

15. Ibid., 4:27-28

16. Ibid., 4:18

17. Ibid., 14: 21-22

18. Ibid., 17:2-7

19. The Traditional Hebrew Text and the New JPS Translation, second Edition, 1999, Deuteronomy 25:5-10

20. The Jesus Dynasty: The Hidden History of Jesus, His Royal Family, and the Birth of Christianity, Simon & Schuster, James Tabor, 2006, 80-81

21. The New English Bible, Oxford University Press, Cambridge University Press, 1970, John 19:25

22. The Jesus Dynasty: The Hidden History of Jesus, His Royal Family, and the Birth of Christianity, Simon & Schuster, James Tabor, 2006, 89.

23. Ibid., 93

24. The New English Bible, Oxford University Press, Cambridge University Press, 1970, Matthew 20:12-13

25. Ibid., John 3:1-6

26. Ibid., Matthew 7:7-8

27. Ibid., Luke 11:9-10

28. The Gospel of Thomas, Stevan Davies, VT, 2002, 5

29. Ibid., 2

30. The New English Bible, Oxford University Press, Cambridge University Press, 1970, Matthew 27:42

31. Ibid., John 15:13

32. The Gospel of Thomas, Stevan Davies, VT, 2002, 15

33. Martin Ling, Muhammad- His life Based on the Earlier Sources, 100

34. Ibid., 101

35. Ibid., 103
36. Ibid., 104
37. Karen Armstrong, Muhammad-a biography of the prophet, New York, 1993, 138
38. Ibid., 140: quote is from in Annemarie Schimmel, And Muhammad is His Messenger-The veneration of the prophet of Islamic piety (Chapel Hill and London, 1985) p. 167-198
39. Ibid., 141-142
40. Hadith of Bukhari, quoted in Harold Rosen, Founders of Faith, the Parallel Lives of God messengers, IL 2010, 313
41. Karen Armstrong, Muhammad-a biography of the prophet, New York, 1993, 142
42. Sachiko Murata and William C. Chittick, The Vision of Islam, MN, 1994, xxv
43. Ibid.

Chapter 7

1. Karen Armstrong, Buddha, New York, 2001, 94
2. Ibid., 95
3. Udana 5:18
4. Thich Nhat Hanh, The heart of the Buddha's teaching, New York, 1999, 51-52
5. Ibid., 59
6. Ibid., 64
7. Ibid., 67
8. Ibid., 113
9. Ibid., 84
10. Ibid., 94-95
11. Ibid., 101
12. Ibid., 105-106
13. Karen Armstrong, Buddha, New York, 2001, 105
14. Babylonian Talmud, *Shabbat* 31a
15. Ibid.
16. The Traditional Hebrew Text and the New JPS Translation, second Edition, 1999, Exodus 22:20
17. Ibid., 20:13-17
18. Zohar 168b

19. The Traditional Hebrew Text and the New JPS Translation, second Edition, 1999, Job 33:28-30
20. Sigmund Freud, The Ego and The Id, NY 1989
21. Rabbi Berg, Reincarnation, Wheels of a Soul, NY 1984, 119-120
22. Rabbi Elie Kaplan Spitz, Does The Soul Survive?, VT 2006, 45-46
23. The Traditional Hebrew Text and the New JPS Translation, second Edition, 1999, Exodus19:5
24. Ibid., 20: 9-10
25. Ibid., 21:2-6
26. Deuteronomy 24:17-19
27. Exodus 22:24
28. The New English Bible, Oxford University Press, Cambridge University Press, 1970, Luke 4:5-7
29. Ibid., Hebrew 2:18
30. Ibid., Luke 16:13
31. Ibid., Luke 4:18-19
32. Ibid., Ibid 4:21
33. Ibid., Matthew 19:19
34. Ibid., Exodus 20:13-17
35. NIV Bible, Luke 6:31
36. Babylonian Talmud, *Shabbat* 31a
37. The New English Bible, Oxford University Press, Cambridge University Press, Luke 6:31
38. Ibid., Luke 6:29-31
39. Ibid., Mark 2:17
40. Ibid., Luke 15:7
41. Ibid, Matthew 5:38
42. Ibid., 5:39
43. Karen Armstrong, Muhammad-a biography of the prophet, New York, 1993, 155
44. Martin Ling, Muhammad- His life Based on the Earlier Sources, 131
45. The Forthy Headith of An-Nawawi's, 13
46. The Koran, Sahin International, *Surat Al-Baqarah (The Cow)* 2:112
47. Karen Armstrong, Muhammad-a biography of the prophet, New York, 1993, 93
48. Ibid., 229

49. The Koran, a New Translation by M.A.S. Abdel Haleem, *(Women)* Sura 4:2-3

50. Karen Armstrong, Muhammad-a biography of the prophet, New York, 1993, 229

51. Michael Newton PhD, Journey of souls-case studies of lives between lives, 85-86

52. Ibid.,127

53. Ibid.

54. Ibid., 145

55. Woman in World History–A Biographical Encyclopedia, Vol. 8, 505-513

56. Michael Newton PhD, Journey of souls-case studies of lives between lives, 169-170

57. Encyclopedia of world biography, Gandhi

About the Author

Ronit Gabay started her spiritual quest back in her birth-land Israel when she graduated cum laude from the David Yellin Academic College of Education in Jerusalem in Bible Studies and History in 1993. In addition, she received an award for her proficiency in the Bible. Her true passion for spirituality was initiated through the process of questioning Judaism, especially in regards to breaking social boundaries. In 2005, Ronit announced her liberation from Judaism and immersed herself in the study of world religions, seeking spiritual meaning beyond religion that would align with her inner truth of oneness.

Today Ronit lives an integrative life in California that is consciously aligned with her spiritual essence, free to be undefined and unlimited.

More information:
RonitGabay.com